Are you interested in

a course management system that would

save you time & effort?

If the answer is *yes*, **CourseCompass is for you.**

**Contact your local
Allyn & Bacon/Longman
sales representative**
for a free access code, or
visit www.coursecompass.com,
and take a tour of this course
management system.

**Technical support
is available for
faculty and students:**
support@coursecompass.com
1-800-677-6337

CourseCompass is an online course management system
designed to help you manage all the aspects of your course –
communication, information distribution, testing and grading.

Let it help you:

- **Communicate directly with your students** via email, discussion boards, and announcement pages.

- **Post documents for your course,** eliminating the need for course packs or handouts.

- **Administer online tests,** with automatic grading and analysis.

- **Provide your students with 24/7 access** to key course information, such as syllabus, assignments, and additional resources – as well as check his/her grade instantly.

Demo CourseCompass today! www.coursecompass.com

Instructor's Manual

for

McKerrow, Gronbeck, Ehninger, and Monroe

Principles and Types
of Public Speaking

Fifteenth Edition

prepared by

Raymie E. McKerrow
Ohio University

Boston   New York   San Francisco
Mexico City   Montreal   Toronto   London   Madrid   Munich   Paris
Hong Kong   Singapore   Tokyo   Cape Town   Sydney

ISBN 0-205-37380-1

Printed in the United States of America

10 9 8 7 6 5 4 3 2   08 07 06 05 04 03 02

ABOUT THIS GUIDE

Principles and Types of Public Speaking is the culmination of the most recent developments in the field of speech communication blended with the basic concepts, principles, and practices which have stood the test of over a half century of classroom use. The overarching goal of the 15th edition is to strengthen those features making this textbook pre-eminent within the field: a commitment to cultural sensitivity with concrete advice to students on how they can talk effectively in a culturally diverse society, and a commitment to the best research base of any basic book in the field. As such, the text retains core concepts which have been its trademark (e.g., Monroe's Motivated Sequence) and leads the field with respect to bringing the best research in both humanistic and social science traditions to bear on the principles and practices of public communication. At the same time, the language of the text continues to be accessible to the entering college undergraduate. Conceptually complex ideas are introduced in a way that makes them both understandable and applicable to the act of speaking in public settings. Furthermore, it is written for students who are computer-literate and who often rely more on Internet sources than paper library sources for their speech materials (and offers contemporary advice on how best to use the Web as a research resource). Developing competent communicators with a sophisticated understanding of public communication is the ultimate goal.

This manual supplements the textbook by offering suggestions for implementing the principles of public speaking in the classroom. It is not intended to be all-inclusive or the final word on using the textbook. It does, however, offer practical ideas for improving the opportunities of your students to master the complex but rewarding process of public speaking. To help you with the various choices that must be made in teaching public speaking, this guide is divided into several sections. The introductory section should be useful in determining some of the available instructional options. More experienced instructors may find it useful as a check for course syllabi, speaking assignments, and other decisions that must be made prior to teaching the basic course.

Next, the focus is shifted to each chapter individually. Detailed teaching strategies for each chapter are provided. Instructional ideas and materials are developed to aid you in presenting the chapter to your students in the most effective manner. Checklists, work sheets, and assessment forms aimed at helping your students make more informed rhetorical choices are included for each chapter. These forms are ready to be duplicated and distributed to your class.

Finally, a selected bibliography provides you with additional sources that might stimulate other instructional choices. The bibliography is divided into several areas including audiovisual resources, general resources on teaching, the assessment of learning, and specific resources in teaching public speaking. You are urged to use this guide as a first step in teaching with the textbook. In combination with materials and activities suggested in the textbook as well as the resources the field of speech communication has to offer, this manual can be an effective tool for you in the basic public speaking course.

Raymie E. McKerrow

CONTENTS

SECTION I: **OVERVIEW: ORGANIZING AND TEACHING**
                        THE BASIC COURSE

A. PLANNING YOUR COURSE

The introductory course in public speaking serves many purposes. First and foremost, it provides students with an understanding of the process of human communication in public situations. The course also alerts students to the complexities involved in making appropriate rhetorical choices in specific situations. Beyond providing a theoretical framework, the course provides students with the opportunity to improve their own skills in preparing and presenting public speeches. Combining theory and practice can be accomplished in a way that provides students with valuable learning experiences in the basic course. This overview is intended to facilitate that planning process.

1. Determining your Goals and Objectives

Knowing where you are going and why is an essential first step in planning day-to-day activities and learning materials. In addition, being sensitive to the students' perspective (reflected in the question "What are we going to learn from this course?") will be helpful. An effective approach is to list the goals and objectives you want to achieve. Daily topics and activities can be evaluated and selected in light of this list. Keep in mind that a variety of activities may facilitate the objectives equally well; there is often no single way to achieve your goals and objectives. The specific choices must be made in light of student interests and needs as well as instructional expertise and preferences. The following discussion may be helpful in determining the goals and objectives you wish to realize through teaching public speaking.

Overall, six things should happen to students in any communication course. According to Bloom's taxonomy of education objectives, they should learn:
> (1) *some facts, theories, methods, technical terms, and principles that constitutes the information or knowledge available from our discipline;*
> (2) *to comprehend, interpret, or translate that information;*
> (3) *to apply that information and their understanding of it in specific situations;*
> (4) *to analyze it by recognizing relationships, deciphering patterns, and identifying forms;*
> (5) *to synthesize the information by developing new relationships or combinations;* (6) *to evaluate it in terms of internal or external criteria.*

Each of these steps functions hierarchically; one step builds upon those preceding it. For example, it is important to know before one can comprehend, to know and comprehend before one can apply, and so on. By way of example, you may decide that an objective of your course is to enhance your student speakers' understanding of their audiences. In order to achieve this overall goal, you identify the factors of attention developed in your textbook (Ch. 8) as key concepts. These decisions plus an understanding of the six steps of learning should guide your development of the material you will teach. An outline of your approach to the key concept, the factors of attention, might look something like this:

Knowledge—ask students to name the factors of attention, list them on the chalkboard, identify them in discussion of current popular television advertisements, or quiz students over the assigned reading.

Comprehension—ask students to explain the relationship of the factors of attention to audience members' interests and desires, and to the speaker's rhetorical choices.

Application—ask students to provide an example of each of the factors of attention.

Analysis—ask students to explain how the factors of attention work in the introduction or conclusion of a speech, or how a speaker decides which factors of attention to use in a particular speech situation.

Synthesis—ask students to develop specific ways audience attention could be stimulated in a real or hypothetical speech situation, to plan an interesting speech on what appears to be a dull topic, or to develop a set of rules or guidelines for the use of each of the factors of attention.

Evaluation—after listening to a student's introduction to a speech, viewing a videotaped speech, or reading a sample speech, ask students whether the factors of attention were well adapted to the mood of the speech (judgment based on internal evidence) and then ask them whether the factors of attention were effective in gaining their attention or if the factors of attention were used as effectively in this speech as in another they have read or viewed (judgment based on external criteria).

The sequence of learning steps sketched in this example should be a useful guide as you decide which specific experiences to use in your classroom. Several other suggestions may also be helpful: As you develop general course objectives, you should remember to determine these objectives based on the needs and abilities of your students. Groups of students vary in abilities, personalities, and background experiences. Your course objectives should accommodate these differences and should be adjusted to meet the special requirements of each group. Because learning is an on-going process, learning objectives should be frequently reassessed. Finally, your objectives should be shared with your students because the task of attaining them is a cooperative venture.

2. Assessing Communication Competencies

The goals and objectives you select should address the basic competencies students should acquire through their experience in a public speaking course. The following list of competencies, while not exhaustive, provides a basic framework for developing your goals.

1.   Understanding the process nature of communication
    A.   Achieved by highlighting the common characteristics shared by interpersonal, small group, and public settings for communication.
    B.   Achieved by examining the interrelated roles of audience, message, and speaker.
    C.   Achieved by focusing on the role of communication in a diverse, democratic society.

2.   Ability to adapt to various speaking situations
    A.   Achieved by requiring both formal (prepared) and informal (impromptu) speaking performances.
    B.   Achieved by requiring speaking performances for a variety of purposes including narration, demonstration, information, persuasion, and special occasion speaking.
    C.   Achieved by promoting an understanding of and techniques for dealing with performance anxiety.

3.   Adaptation to listeners
    A.   Achieved by practicing the modes of gaining and retaining listener attention.
    B.   Achieved by understanding the listening process.
    C.   Achieved by practicing audience analysis.
    D.   Achieved by receiving audience feedback.

4.   Use of argument and logical reasoning
    A.   Achieved by understanding the types of reasoning that may be applied in supporting claims.
    B.   Achieved by recognition and use of claims/propositions of fact, value, and policy.
    C.   Achieved by constructing and defending a case.

5.   Use of supporting materials
    A.   Achieved by requiring citation of external documentation.
    B.   Achieved by requiring the use of a variety of visual aids.
    C.   Achieved by use of statistics, authoritative testimony, etc. as forms of support.

6.   Employing effective organizational strategies in communicating
    A.   Achieved by determining speaking purposes and topics.

      B.   Achieved by understanding and implementing requirements of effective introductions and conclusions.

      C.   Achieved by understanding and using traditional patterns of organization and the motivated sequence.

      D.   Achieved by practicing effective outlining techniques.

7.   Use of motivational speaking skills

      A.   Achieved by practice in adapting language choices and intensity to listeners.

      B.   Achieved by analysis of audience belief and value structures.

      C.   Achieved by implementing the motivated sequence.

      D.   Achieved by determining motive appeals for difference speaking purposes.

8.   Ability to communicate with minimal distractions in vocal and nonverbal delivery

      A.   Achieved by understanding of vocal rate, rhythm, variety, and volume.

      B.   Achieved by practicing vocal delivery adapted to speech purpose.

      C.   Achieved by understanding of physical delivery in eye contact, proxemics, gestures, facial expression, and bodily movement.

      D.   Achieved by using strategies to reduce or control performance anxiety.

9.   Ability to critically evaluate communication

      A.   Achieved by self-analysis of speaking performances including a minimum of one videotaped performance.

      B.   Achieved by instructor evaluation of each speaking performance.

      C.   Achieved by peer evaluations of select speaking performances.

      D.   Achieved by applying the process of rhetorical criticism to select public speaking performances during and outside of class.

For further reading on developing goals and objectives, see: Joan Aitken and Michael Neer, "A Faculty Program of Assessment for a College Level Competency-Based Communicator Core Curriculum," Communication Education 41 (1992): 270-286; Benjamin Bloom, et al., Taxonomy of Educational Objectives: The Classification of Educational Goals (New York: David McKay, 1956).

3. Reaching your Goals and Objectives

The range of specific means to attaining your goals and objectives is limited only by your creativity and the constraints of classroom time and space. The following may be used as a checklist in making decisions.

     Readings—which chapters in the text will be stressed during the term or year? Should students read the chapters in their order of presentation or, if a more suitable organizational scheme suggests itself, how will you assign the textbook chapters? Will you include any supplemental readings and, if so, when will they be used? Will additional supplemental material be needed and how will it be integrated into the textbook material? Will the supplemental readings be required or optional? In particular, how and when will the example speeches in the textbook will be used in the course?

Classroom activities—using in-class exercises (see Assessment Activities at the end of each Chapter) can be a rewarding choice for both instructor and students. Several guidelines will insure that the time spent will not be wasted. You should choose an exercise that is not too complicated or too boring. You also need to consider what you will do if some students finish the task before others; if this is a "get acquainted" activity, students who finish early can just go on talking informally as that also meets your objective. If not, you will need to consider stepping in to manage their talk in more productive ways. Once the exercise or activity is completed, you need to "unpack" it. That is, you should provide students with an understanding of what they have learned during the experience. You may have discussion questions ready; you may tie the exercise into textbook material they have read; you may relate the exercise to a speaking assignment; or you may use the experience as a springboard for a lecture developing additional material. If a group finishes early, you can informally ask them to begin this "integration" process, and call on them in "unpacking" the exercise later in the class session.

Class discussion—good discussions don't just happen; well-prepared instructors nurture and guide them. Good discussion begins by asking questions in a systematic way with an overall guiding purpose or plan. Include questions that ask for specific information, theories, facts, or details (knowledge, comprehension, and application) such as those provided for each chapter of the textbook in the instructional strategies section of this manual. This establishes the basic groundwork for the discussion. You should also ask students to extend their thoughts at the same cognitive level or to move up the hierarchy. This broadens the discussion beyond the level of factual regurgitation to include analysis, synthesis, and evaluation. And, equally important, you should remember to ask students to follow up on their own comments or those of others. You might use standard questions such as, "Would you expand on that?" "Could you provide an example to clarify your answer?" "Why do you think this is the case?" "What would have been another choice in this situation?" During the actual classroom discussion, remember these things: Allow plenty of time for students to think. Pause and be patient as students consider higher level questions. Call on volunteers and occasionally on shy class members to contribute. Be sure to include as many students as possible in the discussion; otherwise you may lose the attention and input of those who are left out. Ask appropriate questions; avoid beginning the discussion with the most difficult question you have prepared; establish the groundwork as well as student interest and willingness to participate with some easier, lower-level questions. Make sure that your question is clearly phrased and understood by everyone. Many times, the failure of students to respond to question is due simply to the way in which the questions are phrased. And, strike a balance between open-ended and specific questions as well as between group and individual questions. For more suggestions on developing questions for classroom discussion, see: Nancy L. Johnson, Active Questioning : Questioning Still Makes the Difference, Creative Learning Consultants, 1996 (ISBN 1880505134); Marylou Dantonio and Paul C. Beisenherz, Learning to Question, Questioning to Learn: Developing Effective Teacher Questioning Practices, Allyn & Bacon, 2000 (ISBN: 0205280366); Nancy L. Johnson, Thinking Is the Key : Questioning Makes the Difference, Creative Learning Consultants, 1992 (ISBN: 1880505010)

Written assignments—you may decide several times during the course of the term to ask students to think carefully about an idea, perhaps do some extra reading or analysis to aid their thoughts, and commit their thoughts to paper. The discussion questions included in this manual and the Assessment Activities at the conclusion of each chapter in the text may provide ideas for such papers. You may ask students to react to or analyze the in-class activities in a short paper. Campus lectures, guest speakers, and various media events provide other triggers for written analysis. You may even ask students to evaluate each others' speaking. Written assignments can introduce students to rhetorical analysis. In providing students with opportunities to practice the criticism of speeches, you should also adequately prepare students for the such a task. Provide guidelines and practice sessions before allowing students to critique each other, especially if the critiques are shared with speakers.

Major speaking assignments—perhaps one of the most important questions you need to ask when planning the basic course, at least from the student's viewpoint, is what primary speaking experiences should be available for your students? Most speaking assignments fall into four broad categories of speaking: narrative, informative, persuasive, and special occasion. To provide your students with a variety of skills you will probably want to include a speaking experience from at least three of these categories. For more ideas on specific assignments for each of the major types of speeches, see the section on speaking assignments in this manual.

Audiovisual resources —there are ample audiovisual resources for teaching the basic course in public speaking. Some of those available are listed in this manual. Your textbook representative can also provide videotapes of sample student speeches and overhead transparencies. Whatever form of audiovisual aid you choose to supplement your classroom teaching, follow the same guidelines suggested in the text. The equipment should supplement your instruction, not be the focus of attention as you attempt to overcome problems with its use. Be prepared for common glitches; have a "plan B" in case something goes wrong with your initial plan, whether that is to use videotapes, PowerPoint slides, or an overhead projector and document camera.

Written feedback—as you record your observations and evaluations of students' performances, attempt to keep your comments timely, balanced, and nonpersonal. That is, provide each student with both praise and constructive suggestions for overcoming the weaknesses in his or her work. Do so within a reasonable period of time following the completion of each assignment. And, avoid making remarks on a personal level such as those directed at things a student cannot change, including personality and physical characteristics. A general rule of thumb when providing written feedback is to think of yourself in your student's place. Most students need to be alerted to their mistakes but also need to receive such information in a supportive manner. This includes suggestions about how to correct their mistakes and an indication of your willingness to discuss their work. Some instructors regularly schedule individual appointments with each student to provide the personal attention students often need.

Once the fundamental decisions about the content of the course have been determined, then the schedule should be developed. Prior to determining the details of the course, the instructor should answer a number of questions about the assignments and the teaching methods chosen. Chief among these: Does each assignment and instructional strategy build upon the skills and knowledge students already possess and provide students with the opportunity to attain even greater proficiency and understanding? It is important that the basic course be more than simply a string of exercises, lectures or practice speeches. It should seek as its primary goal the improvement of the student's communication competence.

B. Developing a Syllabus

Given the diversity of scheduling options that might be used, the purpose of this section is to provide a checklist of items to consider in building a schedule that fits the specific situation you are facing. The sample syllabi are suggestive ways to use the textbook in semester and quarter terms. The syllabus functions as a written contract between you and the student. If you do not specify in advance what attendance means, for example, it will be more difficult to defend your decision to drop a grade due to nonattendance. If you do not specify how you will handle alleged plagiarism, it will be difficult to assess a penalty when such occurs. Thus, the syllabus should cover the basic information as to assignments, reading materials, etc., but should also indicate your criteria for assessing grades, including the impact of attendance and plagiarism on a student's overall standing. Thus, at a minimum, the following information should be included in the syllabus:

Goals/Objectives—what you hope to accomplish should be presented in clear, specific terms. You might list the behavioral objectives or competencies expected.

Textbook(s)—specify all textual materials, including supplemental materials the students may be responsible for, and where they can be obtained if other than through the college bookstore. Place hard to find materials, as well as the course textbook, on reserve at the library.

Tentative Schedule—list the daily schedule of planned activities, including topics, speaking assignments, due dates for written papers, exams, and reading assignments. Since class size may affect when and how much can actually be accomplished, indicating the schedule is tentative allows you to revise based on actual enrollment, etc.

Assignment Guidelines—briefly outline the expectations for each major assignment; you may wish to supplement this with additional information later in the course, but this will give students a basic understanding of what is expected during the term. For exams, indicate the chapters to be covered; if there will be unannounced quizzes, indicate that, as well as how much they will count toward a final grade.

Grading—specify the grading scale for the final course grade as well as the method for reaching a grade on each individual assignment and its weight in the overall course grade. It is important to indicate any penalties for late assignments as well. You may find it helpful to indicate the general criteria for an "A" "B" etc. grade, both for written and oral work.

Contact Information—list your office address, phone number and hours you will be available; also indicate your e-mail address and/or web page. Some guidelines about home phone calls might be included here if that is important.

Attendance—indicate the number of absences permitted and the penalties for missing class. Indicate as well how you will handle missed exams and speeches, since it is inevitable that someone eventually will not be present to deliver a speech or take a scheduled exam. A humane, realistic policy that you can live with is important to establish up front.

Plagiarism—stating your policy in clear terms may avert this unpleasant situation. Provide examples of what is considered plagiarism to guide students in their preparation of assignments. You should explain when sources are cited, how paraphrasing is noted, and what contributions roommates can make in the completion of an assignment. As more students seek information on the Web, you may also want to stress how that material needs to be used and cited.

E-Mail/Web Utilization—if you are creating a listserve for students to use, specify how to sign on, and indicate your expectations for using the list. Indicate whether a web page will be used for further assignment information, etc. If you are using a specific Web resource, such as <u>Blackboard.com</u>, to facilitate interaction indicate how students are to be signed in, and what your expectations are for chat room use, etc.

Research—if students in the basic course are used as subjects in communication research, you should note how their participation or non-participation will be handled. A university-wide policy on the use of human subjects may guide you in this area.

Resources—a bibliography of additional readings or outside sources in the area of communication might simplify the task of extra credit assignments or stimulate students to further investigate the discipline.

Special Instructions/Requirements—this is a "catch-all" category for any additional information the students should be aware of in meeting the course objectives. The time and room assignment for the final exam and broad guidelines for speech topics, such as they must be in good taste or must adhere to all local legal statutes, might be specified.

Even though the specific reading assignments, speeches, and instructional strategies will vary, a skeletal syllabus may provide some ideas for organizing the daily routine in the basic course. The following schedules assume approximately 25 students per class and allow for up to 6 major speaking assignments. If less formal student performance is desired, speaking days can be easily replaced with lectures, discussions or exercises. Since mass lecture courses and individual contract grading have special requirements in terms of resources and planning, they have not been considered. Each is a viable alternative to the small classroom setting and the materials in the next sections of this manual can be adapted to fit those special circumstances.

FIFTEEN WEEK SCHEDULE----THREE MEETINGS PER WEEK

This course schedule can be adapted to a 10 week course providing there are 4 class meetings or two two-hour meetings per week (40 class hours with each day below as one class hour). If that is the case, you will need to compress lecture discussion time before and after Speech 5 to get a 6th speech in the schedule.

Day 1	Orientation/Get acquainted exercise	
Day 2	Lecture/discussion/exercise	(readings)
Day 3	Lecture/discussion/exercise	(readings)
Day 4	Speech #1 (2-3 minutes)	
Day 5	Speech #1	
Day 6	Lecture/discussion/exercise	(readings)

Day 7	Lecture/discussion/exercise	(readings)
Day 8	Lecture/discussion/exercise	(readings)
Day 9	Speech #2 (3-5 minutes)	
Day 10	Speech #2	
Day 11	Speech #2	
Day 12	Speech #2	
Day 13	Lecture/discussion/exercise	(readings)
Day 14	Lecture/discussion/exercise	(readings)
Day 15	Lecture/discussion/exercise	(readings)
Day 16	Speech #3 (4-6 minutes)	
Day 17	Speech #3	
Day 18	Speech #3	
Day 18	Speech #3	
Day 19	Lecture/discussion/exercise	(readings)
Day 20	Lecture/discussion/exercise	(readings)
Day 21	Lecture/discussion/exercise---Midterm examination	
Day 22	Lecture/discussion/exercise	(readings)
Day 23	Speech #4 (4-6 minutes)	
Day 24	Speech #4	
Day 25	Speech #4	
Day 26	Speech #4	
Day 27	Lecture/discussion/exercise	(readings)
Day 28	Lecture/discussion/exercise	(readings)
Day 29	Lecture/discussion/exercise	(readings)
Day 30	Lecture/discussion/exercise	(readings)
Day 31	Speech #5 (5-7 minutes)	
Day 32	Speech #5	
Day 33	Speech #5	
Day 34	Speech #5	
Day 35	Speech #5	
Day 36	Lecture/discussion/exercise	(readings)
Day 37	Lecture/discussion/exercise	(readings)
Day 38	Lecture/discussion/exercise	(readings)
Day 39	Lecture/discussion/exercise	(readings)
Day 40	Speech #6 (5-7 minutes)	
Day 41	Speech #6	
Day 42	Speech #6	
Day 43	Speech #6	
Day 44	Speech #6	
Day 45	Lecture/discussion/exercise---Final examination	

FIFTEEN WEEK SCHEDULE----TWO MEETINGS PER WEEK

This course schedule also works well for 6 week sprint courses or summer terms which are 6 or 8 weeks in length.

Day 1	Orientation/Get acquainted activity	
Day 2	Lecture/discussion/exercise	(readings)
Day 3	Speech #1	
Day 4	Lecture/discussion/exercise	(readings)
Day 5	Lecture/discussion/exercise	(readings)
Day 6	Speech #2	
Day 7	Speech #2	
Day 8	Lecture/discussion/exercise	(readings)
Day 9	Lecture/discussion/exercise	(readings)
Day 10	Speech #3	
Day 11	Speech #3	
Day 12	Speech #3	
Day 13	Lecture/discussion/exercise	(readings)
Day 14	Lecture/discussion/exercise	(readings)
Day 15	Speech #4	
Day 16	Speech #4	
Day 17	Speech #4	
Day 18	Lecture/discussion/exercise	(readings)
Day 19	Lecture/discussion/exercise	(readings)
Day 20	Speech #5	
Day 21	Speech #5	
Day 22	Speech #5	
Day 23	Speech #5	
Day 24	Lecture/discussion/exercise	(readings)
Day 25	Lecture/discussion/exercise	(readings)
Day 26	Speech #6	
Day 27	Speech #6	
Day 28	Speech #6	
Day 29	Speech #6	
Day 30	Lecture/discussion/exercise----Final examination	

C. Speaking Assignments

As suggested earlier, you will want to include experiences from at least three of the major categories of speeches. This provides a well-rounded variety of in-class speaking practice for students, preparing them for the potential variety of speech situations they will encounter during the remainder of their college years and future careers. The following suggestions are grouped according to the general type of speech experience. They provide orientations to basic speech assignments and springboards to assignment variations. Be sure to consult the suggestions in each chapter for further ideas for speaking assignments.

The First Speech—most often, the first formal speaking assignments stress limited content development such as a single idea or demonstration. Students are usually concerned with problems of delivery including posture, gestures, eye contact, use of note cards, and above all, coping with communication anxiety. Because speaking is such a new experience, many instructors choose to limit the length of these first speeches. Often, two to four minutes is enough time to develop a single idea adequately and introduce the student to the speaking experience. In preparation for the first speech, student should certainly be acquainted with the basic elements in the speech communication process and suggestions for overcoming stage fright. Speakers should also know how to choose and narrow topics which are appropriate for the speech occasion. The initial chapters in your textbook are an excellent foundation for the first speech. You may also want to introduce students to the basic organizational patterns and the requirements for good introductions and conclusions.

Minimum assignment objectives for this speech are clear vocal delivery with limited disfluencies, nondistracting physical delivery including frequent eye contact with listeners, and a clearly communicated single, central idea. Variations on this assignment are practically unlimited. One possibility is to ask students to explain the importance an aphorism or 'rule for living' has for them, or should have for others. You might ask students to talk about themselves or another member of the class whom they have interviewed or a person who has been influential in their lives. To aid students in narrowing their topics, some instructors ask them to focus on their home towns, their majors, a memorable event in their lives, or their favorite pet. You may introduce a supporting material component in this assignment by asking students to find out more about their hometown, the day they were born, a hero or heroine, or even the history of a word or phrase.

Narrative Speaking—the narrative speech involves telling a story, providing your listeners with some insight by placing them vicariously in the situation. Speakers often relate an experience which illustrates a moral or principle. This objective may require them to present a series of events to their listeners in chronological order. It is usually an excellent early assignment since the pattern of organization is predetermined and a central idea is developed. This allows students to continue to master physical and vocal delivery as well as to channel communication apprehension. The narrative speech can form the basis of an introduction to the use of supporting material, particularly illustration, specific instances, and comparison/contrast. Prior to this assignment you should acquaint students with the principles of narrative or chronological organization, physical and vocal delivery, and the essential features of informative speaking. You may also include material on language strategies and audience analysis.

Minimum objectives for the narrative speech are similar to those for the first speech, although the expectations for delivery should be somewhat higher. Student speakers should be able to develop a central idea and state it clearly for listeners. They should also be able to choose relevant details that enhance the purpose and mood of the narrative. They should utilize a conversational rate and style of delivery, free from distracting mannerisms, both vocal and physical. You might also ask that they use their delivery to emphasize ideas and enhance the mood of the narration such as indicating characters or plot changes through vocal characteristics or physical movement.

Variations of this assignment include asking students to present or read non-original material such as short stories or poetry. They might reconstruct an episode of a novel, film, or television program from the perspective of a single character. They could narrate the events of the most embarrassing or exciting moment of their lives. Students can exercise their creative ability in developing their own fairy tales or "one-minute" bedtime stories. To add a research dimension to this assignment, an historical event such as a famous battle or daily life in a medieval castle could be recreated in narrative form. Students can also be asked to report on assigned topics, such as language development in children or famous speakers from history, or provide oral instructions, such as directions to a location on campus.

Informative Speaking—the informative series of speeches requires more complex organizational and research skills. Usually by this point, students have been introduced to the use of supporting material to enhance speaker credibility. Certainly they should be encouraged to read and utilize the chapter on informative speaking. In addition, you may choose to add visual aids in this speech assignment.

Minimum assignment objectives include the use of orally cited external evidence to add to speaker credibility. Students should choose an organizational pattern appropriate for their speech topic and use internal previews, transitions, and summaries. They should also demonstrate an adequate understanding of what audience members already know and adapt their speech to that level of knowledge. An optional criterion is the use of a well prepared visual aid to enhance the speech content. To complete this assignment you may ask students to prepare a demonstration, oral report, or lecture. Their information may take the form of a biographical sketch, demonstration of a complex process, or explanation of a theory found in their major or another discipline. Students could tackle concepts or abstract terms, defining them for the audience. They might provide directions for completing tasks or take their audience on an imaginary guided tour of an historical site. The variations are endless and can easily be adapted to the interests of both speaker and audience.

Problem-Solution Speeches—problem-solution speeches can be used as a bridge between informative and persuasive speaking. Problem-solution speeches require the development of a problem using the skills of informative speaking and the presentation of a viable solution utilizing the skills of persuasive speaking. Since this assignment integrates the functions of informative and persuasive speaking, it provides a good introduction to both persuasive and more focused argumentative speaking.

Students should be alerted to the special organizational requirements of problem-solution speeches. Clear substructure becomes very important in problem-solution speeches because both the problem and the solution must be developed in detail. You might ask students to provide reasons the problem exists or reasons the solution is the best alternative to solving the problem. This gives students practice in developing rudimentary arguments. As you assess this speech assignment, you should pay particular attention to the speaker's attempt to make the problem relevant to the audience as well as the viability of the suggested solution. The solution should be workable, based on realistic plans and financing. It should be fully developed, not simply, "Write your congressional representative." And, it should solve the problems developed in the early part of the speech.

Persuasive and Argumentative Speaking—the persuasion assignment offers multiple opportunities for creativity and a chance for students to refine skills in audience analysis, motivational appeals, and argumentation. Since this assignment requires mastery of delivery, organization, and audience analysis skills, it should not be attempted until students have satisfactorily completed earlier assignments. The textbook chapters on speaking to persuade and argue provide important foundations for this assignment. You may want to review concepts such as audience analysis and supporting material as well.

Minimum objectives for persuasive and argumentative speaking should include the ability to develop and effectively combine basic arguments and motivational appeals. Students should also adapt their delivery to suggest sincere and enthusiastic personal involvement or conviction. Listeners' attention should be maintained and they should be able to follow the development of the speech content easily. Persuasive speeches can be adapted to varied audiences, past, present or future, or to special speech purposes such as sales. They might also be refutative as in debates and pro-con speeches, one-sided and two-sided, or question-answer sessions. The entire class can be involved in speaking through a mock legislative body or a moot court setting. Several forms have been provided in this manual for other kinds of persuasive assignments including the policy change speech and attitudinal reinforcement speech.

The Special Occasion Speech—the special occasion assignment can be based on the forms discussed in the textbook chapter or variations of those forms. One popular variation is the career speech, in which the student plays a role from a potential future career or explains aspects of that career to the classroom audience. This general speaking assignment encourages students to become more sensitive to audience expectations and demands of the occasion. It also requires an understanding of the elements of informative and persuasive speaking--a reason most instructors schedule this assignment after the basics of informative and persuasive speaking have been covered. In place of the more traditional special occasions such as Martin Luther King's birthday, Flag Day, or Halloween, you may wish to substitute a local observance or even create your own special occasion such as "Public Speaker's Day" or "Communication Week." To set the mood, you might reserve a special room on campus for the speeches. Sometimes, moving from the classroom into a banquet room or a conference center can foster the atmosphere of a special occasion.

Since this assignment follows others, it should show improvement in one or more of the basic skills attempted in previous speaking assignments. It should also reveal the student's ability to recognize and adapt speaking purpose, organization, logical and motivational appeals, and delivery to the special audience and situation of the occasion.

Speaking at Conferences or Meetings—students should be able, toward the end of the term, to implement many of the communication skills that are critical for effective speaking in a setting such as a conference or small group meeting. They should be able to adapt to the interaction required for an efficient and effective group experience. Assignments can be formulated to include keynote presentations before a large group, or panel presentations as part of a smaller group. In the former instance, the keynote should illustrate the student's ability to focus attention on what can be gained from the conference; in the latter instance, interacting effectively with other members of the group becomes a key criterion for success.

Speaking Portfolios—since your primary goal during the public speaking course is to develop skills based on an understanding of the communication process, your students should be able to demonstrate mastery over basic competencies at the end of the term. You might require that students prepare a convincing case of their skill level. A portfolio allows students to gather materials throughout the quarter or semester. Their portfolio might include speech outlines, videotapes of polished speech performances, evaluations from others, and other evidence that they have achieved proficiency in communication. The portfolio offers several advantages over traditional single assignments. It focuses students on their overall accomplishments and asks them to find evidence demonstrating what they have achieved. It stresses a holistic, rather than fragmented, approach to the

15

course content. In addition, a completed portfolio often provides a convincing argument for potential employers.

As this section suggests, there are a variety of ways to accomplish your objectives in teaching a public speaking course. Assignments that are clearly explained and targeted to achieving the course's objectives will be much easier to implement. Assignments that capture and retain student interest also will make for a more pleasant experience for both you and the students. Students achieve at the level of expectations set; making assignment objectives clear, and indicating how improvement will be monitored and evaluated will also make the evaluation process much easier to communicate in assessing specific grades for speeches. There should be a clearly discernible progression of development of skills and observable improvement demonstrated by students.

D. Helping Students find Speaking Topics

More often than not, topic selection is the most difficult task facing a student. Several classroom applications can aid in stimulating creative and varied student speech topics. In addition, an instructor's attention to the process of finding appropriate speech topics will direct students' attention to the importance of this step in the process of developing a speech.

Brainstorming—working alone or as part of a small group, this process allows students to list as many topics as they can think of, without evaluating their utility or interest. Either as a large group or as individuals, students can practice the principles of brainstorming to discover topics. The list is limited only by the ingenuity of students in your class. Collect the lists and collate them before the next class. You can evaluate their workability, and indicate the kinds of topics preferred or expected when you review the collated list with your class.

Checklists—provide a list of questions for students to answer about their hobbies, values, interests, courses being taken, etc. Such checklists can trigger ideas that students might not have otherwise discovered. The Topic Selection Checklist included in this manual performs this function.

Contemporary issues—ask students to listen to the news or read a major news source for several days before the exercise, then discuss how current controversies can provide topics for further development in speeches. Or students can be required to bring several different newspapers and magazines to class. From the articles in these news sources, general and specific speech topics and purposes can be discovered.

Narrowing from general ideas—begin with a broad general topic area such as human rights, pollution, or freedom. List related topics and/or narrow each until students are able to distinguish between broad and narrow topic areas.

Assignment linked topics—some topics are better suited to particular types of speech assignments:

Speech Using a Visual Aid:
>   Pollution hazards in your county (local focus)
>   Clean water resources in the nation (national focus)
>   Upper atmosphere wind currents (international scope)

Informative Speech:
>   University efforts to improve diversity (local focus)
>   Bio-hazards in a post 9/11 age (national focus)
>   Terrorism and Islam (international scope)

Problem-Solution Speech:
>   Recycling in your city (local focus)
>   Providing health care to all children (national focus)
>   U.S. acid rain and its effects in Canada (international scope)

Two-Sided Persuasion:
>   Should we ban the use of hazardous farm chemicals in our state? (local issue)
>   Do we need stricter U.S. standards for sewage disposal? (national issue)
>   What can we do to heal the divisions in Israel/Palestine? (international issue)

Precedents/Taboos—provide students with a list of speech topics from previous terms that have been used successfully. Discuss the possibilities and limitations of each topic. In addition, some instructors dislike particular topics ("how to put a clarinet together" might be an example; "how to saddle a horse"–with the animal in the room [it has been done!!] might be another). In fairness, students should have an idea of the "taboo" topics–this may also generate a discussion on why they are not encouraged, or what might be done to overcome the concerns over their development as a topic. Ask for variations on topics and suggestions for more creative approaches.

Individual conferences—some instructors require that students get prior approval for their speech topics. This has the advantage of encouraging student interaction with the instructor. It also discourages those students who procrastinate in their research and development of a speech. It offers every student the advantage of direct feedback from the instructor.

After the topics have been suggested and listed, it is important for the instructor to aid in winnowing ideas for speech topics. In this process it is advisable to discuss the nature of the general purpose of the speech and the specific purpose as well as audience expectations and rhetorical sensitivity. You might suggest the following guidelines for choosing topics:

1. *Does the topic fit the general purpose of the speech assignment?* For example, students occasionally forget that their general purpose is to inform or persuade rather than perform or entertain. In their desire to please their classmates, entertainment may replace another speaking purpose.

2. *Does the topic fit the specific assignment parameters?* If this speech is limited to 5 minutes, can you cover the topic adequately in that amount of time? Is information readily available? Is the topic fresh and interesting without being trivial or distorted?

3. *Is the topic suitable for an educated audience?* That is, while occasionally silly exercises and classroom activities lighten the atmosphere, the major assignments should reflect a genuine effort to reach academically respectable heights. Choosing scholarly/serious approach to topic development also reflects the speaker's appreciation of the classroom audience as an educated one. Rather than underestimating their intelligence with cute but underdeveloped speech topics such as "Housebreaking a Hamster," "Repotting a Plant," or "Mixing a Drink," speakers can fulfill their responsibilities as an effective speaker. As an instructor, you can add to their knowledge and make your public speaking course an outstanding forum for the presentation of critical issues. As suggested earlier, this is one reason you may want to cull from topic suggestions a list of "off-limit" topics that students should rise above, or at the very least be more creative in establishing a reason for hearing a speech on such a topic.

In the best tradition of a liberal arts education, focusing on discovery of ideas for speaking can stimulate and develop students' growing interest in the world around them. It also ensures that the speeches presented during the term reflect careful thought and insight. It requires that students investigate the possibilities of a topic using the best resources they can locate before they address their classmates. This approach offers students an opportunity to delve deeply into a topic and enhances their understanding of their world.

E. Handling Student Communication Anxiety

Perhaps one of the most common and difficult things for students in the beginning public speaking course is their first encounter with communication anxiety. Students rarely report feeling completely comfortable speaking before peers. The usual reaction is to express discomfort which ranges from mild embarrassment to outright panic. You can prepare students to cope with the manifestations of anxiety. Some of the preparation is indirect. For example, it is helpful if students feel their classmates understand and are sympathetic. Often, this is achieved by cultivating a positive, reinforcing class atmosphere and by giving students an early opportunity to get to know some of their classmates through small group interaction. More directly, pointing out that some anxiety may well be a positive sign of the student's sincere interest in doing well will help to allay fears that being anxious is not a good thing.

It is important that you understand the anxiety process and be ready to intervene more actively when extreme anxiety occasionally occurs in an individual student. A useful way to think about anxiety is as a process of moving from the initial stimuli that provokes anxious feelings to its possible remediation. The stress-inducing stimuli occurs in some form, such as being called upon to speak in class. The automatic physiological reaction to this stimuli is adrenalin arousal. The body responds by readying itself for flight--the heartbeat quickens, breathing becomes more rapid and shallow, palms sweat, blushing occurs, and so on. This situation is mentally recognized as anxiety and the mind is prepared to react defensively. Usually this stage is accompanied by the occurrence of negative self-statements. In this phase of the anxiety spiral, a speaker thinks: "They don't like me," "I'm going to fail," or "I should have practiced more." The process begins anew when these negative self-statements act as additional stressors encouraging further physiological reactions. The case of nerves begins to intensify if the cycle is not interrupted. Besides informing students about the process and its affects on them, you can actively help students intervene to break the cycle of anxiety. You can suggest physical and mental responses to reduce the impact of anxiety:

> *Physical responses*—develop and utilize exercises such as deep breathing, isometrics, and others; practice progressive relaxation or systematic desensitization.

> *Mental responses*—reappraise the nature of the stimuli causing anxiety. Students often make themselves more anxious by preparing to be nervous and confronting their responses with feelings of being suddenly overwhelmed. If they are aware that they sometimes actually practice and reinforce their own anxiety, they can avoid doing so. It is important to stress the positive especially when in an arousal state; save the negative until arousal subsides. Self-reinforcement with positive statements is valuable. This might include statements such as "Some anxiety is normal" or "I really know this speech and believe in what I'm saying." Students should write and practice replacement statements so an arsenal is ready. Finally, have students set realistic goals. It is likely that students set themselves up to feel anxious by putting undue emphasis on a speech. They might be internalizing thoughts such as: "I have to get an A on this speech or my grades will be so bad, I'll lose my scholarship." The normal stress of the speaking situation is heightened by superhuman ambitions.

While each of these strategies for intervention in the anxiety spiral is useful, it is important to recognize the degree of anxiety and work with it. Since anxiety is a relative and elusive concept, this is sometimes a difficult task. The key in dealing with student anxiety is to maximize their performance by coping with the blocks preventing positive performance. There are many evaluative instruments, including the common self-report test for communication apprehension, the Personal Report of Communication Anxiety or PRCA, can be found in James C. McCroskey, <u>An Introduction to Rhetorical Communication</u>, 4th ed. Englewood Cliffs, NJ: Prentice-Hall, 1982.

F. Critical Thinking Skills

What is critical thinking? Why should we teach students to think critically? These questions have recently begun to surface as the result of renewed interest not only in teaching students facts and ideas, but in teaching them the thinking skills they will need to handle new information and ideas in the future. Born in an age of technological and information explosions, our students cannot hope to learn all the facts they will need in their lifetimes during several short years of college education. But, if we teach them how to approach and assimilate new bodies of information, they will have the skills necessary for mastering the sea of new information they will confront.

We know from research in education that critical thinking skills can be taught and that most students, including those who traditionally enroll in lower level courses, can reap the benefits of a critical thinking orientation in our approach to teaching. The process of critical thinking is one which encourages students to integrate course content, their own experiences, and the wisdom of others into a harmonious whole. Critical thinking occurs as the student grapples head-on with ideas rather than memorizing sterile units of information. A comparison of those students who successfully solve problems by integrating information with those who fail to solve problems effectively yields clear differences. Those students who employ successful problem-solving or critical thinking behaviors have these characteristics in common:

1.   *Selective attention.*

2.   *Perseverence in understanding a problem fully.*

3.   *Comparing the known with the unknown; drawing appropriate analogies between the familiar and the unfamiliar.*

4.   *Reserve judgment until all available factors have been considered.*

5.   *Construct and pre-test solutions before final commitment is made.*

These bases of thinking critically are skills. Like any other skill, they can and should be taught and learned in our public speaking classrooms. This manual has already presented ideas about developing goals, using questions, and designing assignments to stimulate critical thinking. Specific questions designed to stimulate critical thinking are included for each chapter in the instructional strategies section of this manual. Your textbook further develops critical thinking as an essential component in argumentation. You also can check out the Critical Thinking Assessment Project

at California State University, Chico [http://www.csuchico.edu/phil/ct/ct_assess.htm#comps] for further tools in working with critical thinking. In terms of your present course, here are some additional suggestions:

1.   *Ask students to keep an individual speech file for present and future use*. The file should be prepared so that it will serve as a nucleus for expanded information on core topics as well as additional topics. Library and web-based research skills can be incorporated as students add notes on relevant reading. Organization, argumentation, audience analysis, and language skills can also be utilized if students are asked to jot notes in their files about potential ways to develop and adapt their speech material. This file might replace individual assignment sheets for classroom speeches or the daily speech journal.

2.   *Provide or have students generate a group-based or class-based topic around which all assignments would revolve*. See Lawrence W. Hugenberg and Daniel J. O'Neill, "Speaking on Critical Issue Topics in the Public Speaking Course," The Speech Communication Teacher 2 (1987): 12-13.

3.   *Have students prepare an oral or written critical analysis of a presentation by an outside speaker, a national public address, or a published speech text*. Audience members or readers should be provided with arguments and supporting material in an attempt to persuade them to accept the speaker's final evaluation.

4.   *Create 3-4 member peer groups to provide feedback following speeches*. Their discussion should focus on the speeches of each group member, reinforcing positive progress and offering constructive suggestions for coping with each speaker's limitations. To obtain maximum results, it is important that the task dimension of these groups and to concentrate on the development of each group member. For this reason, the group should be supervised and meet regularly.

5.   *Create 2-4 person student groups to quiz each other over chapter concepts*. Have them identify differences of opinion/understanding and then use those as part of an overall class review before the next exam. The groups also could develop a competitive quiz game in which teams compete. This student-oriented approach to course content review is further developed by Paul Chance in an article summarizing Benjamin Bloom's revolutionary approach to education (see reference list at end of Section 1).

6.   *Use multiple media to stimulate creative approaches to concepts*. Visual and auditory media contribute, not only to longer term retention of material, but also to understanding material in new frameworks. Media can encourage students' use of multiple senses in

approaching and solving problems. A series of media programs are available from your textbook representative for use with this textbook including videotapes of classroom speeches and overhead transparencies. Each of these media can form the springboard for a discussion of chapter concepts or assignments.

G. Assessing Student Performance

The ultimate goal of assessment should be to improve student learning. The best approach to assessment involves multiple measures and formats for collecting input over a period of time. Ultimately, however, students and instructors both realize that the student will receive a final course grade–a single number or letter which signifies their total accomplishments during the time they have spent in class. This symbol holds a myriad of emotional and valuative overtones for the student, the parent, the future employer or graduate institution, and even, the course instructor. Given the fact that most institutions require some kind of grading scale be employed in assessing student performance, it is beneficial to face the problem head-on, setting standards, reviewing procedures, and establishing the general framework for student evaluation. With these purposes in mind, let us examine several areas of evaluation.

1. Critiquing Speeches

The evaluative process used in appraising speeches is subjective. This is not to say that it is arbitrary and capricious as a result. Adherence to a number of basic guidelines should make the process of evaluating speeches at least more consistent if not a more conscious process. At least five general guidelines are necessary. You may find it helpful to add others.

> *Develop clear general criteria for assessment*—share these generously with your students. (The Criteria for Grading Form included in Chapter Two is included in this manual). Both you and the student should understand and recognize the distinctions between an A performance and a B performance as well as among the other grade levels. For your legal protection, standards for plagiarism, attendance, missing assigned speaking days, the availability of make-up exams or speaking times, and any other special conditions you wish to have students adhere to must be given to each student in written form. In developing your general criteria for grading, you will need to stick closely to your own guidelines, putting them in concrete form and reminding yourself frequently so they do not fluctuate from one class period to the next. It is important to demonstrate consistency in grading to retain your students' faith in your fairness and ability to discern among the varieties of performance in your class. It is often a good idea to review the criteria for a speaking assignment and the objectives you hope to attain with it prior to grading/listening to a series of speeches. Another good check on your consistency is to keep a short log of each speaker, topic, main weaknesses and strengths, or, if you type comments, keep a file for each student and read through the prior evaluation before you

begin the next one. If the speaker improves dramatically during the course of the term, then your grades should probably reflect this improvement. The opposite is also true. In addition, you can see from the log whether or not you emphasize one element of speaking to the exclusion of others, if you change your expectations to fit the nature of the assignments, or if you tend to grade too easily or too harshly. Perhaps the most important aspect of a multi-sectioned basic course with several instructors teaching and evaluating students is to establish some inter-rater reliability. Staff meetings which offer the opportunity to discuss elements of evaluation, comparison of final or in-progress grades, and the sharing of critique forms may alert instructors to the need to bolster or loosen their grading standards. Practice sessions can also be beneficial for instructors. Several live or taped speakers should be evaluated by each instructor then the rating shared and discussed.

Establish specific grading strategies—prior to each assignment provide your students with the total percentage of the final grade and the specific points awarded for the speech. You may find it helpful to break the points into categories such as 10 points possible for the introduction, 20 for supporting material, 30 for delivery, and so on. This should aid students as they prepare for the assignment and it will show them where their strengths and weaknesses lie when they have completed the assignment. In addition, it provides a concrete set of standards for the instructor. The task of counseling a student is made easier if the grade has been justified in this way. If a letter grade rather than points is used, you will probably need to indicate more specifically (in written comments) the overall strengths and weaknesses of the speech.

Balance your evaluation—in critiquing assignments, provide a mixture of both positive comments and suggestions for improvement. Students almost always appreciate suggestions of ways to improve their speaking and they like lots of response to their speaking. If you are not filling most of the available area on the average speech critique form, you probably need to be responding more fully to students. If you are using the back of the critique form because you have run out of room on the front, you probably have a classroom full of grateful students, especially if you balance your comments well. Even the worst student speaker has probably done something worth noting in a favorable light and certainly the best student speaker in your class has not yet reached perfection. They need to know these reactions to help set their personal standards for improvement on the next assignment and to maintain the achievements they have already made. One strategy to improve balance, and to guard against overreacting to a speaker's performance, is to make notes during class, and then rework those into a more formal evaluation of strengths and weaknesses before the next class.

Keep good records—unless you plan to file copies of each student's work throughout the semester (an expensive and cumbersome task at best), you need to keep excellent records of grades, attendance, performances on in-class activities, and other things pertinent to your final evaluation. The system you use is not as important as the thoroughness and accuracy of your records. You probably never realize this as much as when, several terms later, a student challenges a grade or asks you to check for a mathematical error.

2. Testing

In treating the subject of written evaluations, numerous specific suggestions are available on the formulation of exam items, the validity and reliability of written examinations, and the replacement of traditional exams with innovative evaluations. Due to this abundance of material on the topic, this manual will not attempt to replicate the details of planning and executing various examinations. However, some basic guidelines regarding examinations in the public speaking course should be noted:

1. *Keep the focus in the exam on communication-relevant concepts and situations.*

2. *Keep the verbal difficulty of the items low or average in relation to the group which is to take the test, unless its purpose is to measure verbal and reading skills.*

3. *Avoid taking statements verbatim from the text to create test items.*

4. *Avoid trick questions or even the appearance of them.*

5. *Double-check to see that one item does not provide cues to the answer of another item or items.*

6. *In multiple choice tests, use a random correct response pattern rather than a systematic pattern.*

7. *Vary the difficulty level of the items.* The lower levels of difficulty draw upon the knowledge, comprehension, and application levels of Bloom's educational taxonomy while the more difficult items stress analysis, synthesis, and evaluation.

8. *Indicate how you will resolve conflicts over questions or answers.* A formal appeal system should be developed for multi-section courses.

3. Keeping, Accessing Exam Files

Instructors often find it helpful to develop files of examination items over the course of several terms. This practice not only allows you to compare student performance on various examination items, but makes the best use of good examination items. Among the several formats available for the examination file, the index card system and the computerized data bank are popular. Whether you keep your examination items in a steel card file or on a diskette, you should record the question itself, the question type (true-false, multiple choice, essay, etc.), the answer, the page reference in the textbook, the difficulty level, the terms the item was used, and statistical data such as percent answer correctly and hi-low item analysis if it is available. As noted in the list of Ancillaries (see textbook, following Preface) Allyn & Bacon maintains a Test bank and computerized file for your use in constructing exams.

H. Facilitating Learning in the Classroom

Research has shown that students, regardless of intellectual capacity, approach learning tasks in very different ways. Experienced instructors already know, and first-time instructors soon learn, that while you can teach the same course content over and over, it is never really the same course. No two groups of students are ever the same. The tendency to assume that all students are basically alike should be resisted. Typically, we employ a certain teaching style and methods compatible with that style in direct contradiction to our recognition that there are important differences among learners (see McKerrow, 1998 in references at the end of this section). By selecting teaching techniques that match the learning styles of students, you can create the best possible learning environment for a group of students. By doing so you may also prevent your classroom from becoming provincial, structurally stagnant, and psychologically simplistic.

What specific differences should you consider as you adapt to your students? How can you identify these differences? And, what are the implications for your course design once you identify variations among learners? Space does not permit an extensive answer to these questions, but some basic suggestions for further investigation will be attempted.

Recognizing other ways of learning, and valuing them in their own right, is a key element in differentiating student approaches to the content and performance dimensions of this course. Gardner (1988) has posited seven "intelligences" that, collectively, inhabit the person if not always the student. The first two are the most common, as they are associated with SAT and other "IQ" measures. That is, they are the academy as we experience and value it

> *Linguistic*—poetic expression may be the epitome of this intelligence in its finest moments.

> *Logical*—predominantly associated with mathematical and scientific abilities.

> *Spatial*—mental models of a "universe" and manipulation of that world is highlighted here -- sailors, engineers, surgeons, sculptors, painters are notable.

Musical—ability to manipulate sound in ways that make for aesthetically pleasing creations; think of a Mozart or a Bernstein.

Bodily—kinesthetic skill, to use one's body in creative ways to solve problems; think of athletes, dancers, surgeons.

Interpersonal—the ability to understand and relate to other people; think of salespeople, teachers, clinicians, religious leaders, politicians.

Intrapersonal—correlative to interpersonal, but turned inward; understand oneself accurately and use that knowledge effectively in decision-making.

Valuing any one of these as most important or essential leads to errors in judgment. Gardner (1988) suggests, for example, that valuing logical thinking above all can manifest itself in the errors of the "best and the brightest"--when Harvard's best brought on the Vietnam conflict in the Kennedy administration. The same error is made if one assumes that only those intelligences readily "testable" are important or crucial. The only thing that the analogy "PERFIDIOUS is to TREACHERY as AUDACIOUS is to (a) FEAR, (b) COURAGE, (c) HONESTY, (d) MENDACITY may tell us is that a student's vocabulary lacks such terms (Sternberg, 1988) (this section adapted from McKerrow, 1998).

Once the variety of student learning styles has been assessed, you can develop a range of instructional strategies that meet the needs of most, if not all, of the individual students in a class. Students can also benefit through gaining greater insight into their own learning styles. They can make more informed decisions about how to best adapt to different classroom environments and tap their learning strengths. Perhaps the best rule in recognizing varied learning and teaching styles is to remain flexible. Rather than prescribing specific learning activities, you and your students should both be open to experiment. A blend of methods and alternatives to accommodate individual differences may be the best approach to teaching and learning.

I. Improving your Teaching

Finally, it is important to note that although countless textbook manuals have been developed and distributed, the ultimate determinant of the course quality and thus the learning experience of the student is you. Many educators agree that improving as an instructor is a process that can be encouraged in a variety of ways. The following suggestions offer a beginning. The important thing to remember when you decide that you want to become a better teacher is that the process is one of discovery--discovering things about yourself and about the course you are teaching. Hopefully, these suggestions will stimulate that process of discovery:

Watch others teach—observe teachers you consider to be excellent as well as those you think are mediocre or poor. What are the differences you see among them? What distinguishes one person's teaching style from another? What attitudes toward students and course content do they convey? List the teaching strategies that you might adapt to your teaching.

Consider your students' evaluations—both formal and informal student reactions to your teaching and the course can be helpful. Many departments require some kind of evaluation at the end of a term, with the form administered by someone other than you. Are students comfortable talking with you? Are you able to explain ideas so that they can be fully grasped? Do students consider you to be fair and reasonable in your expectations? Keep in mind that this does not necessarily mean that you are too easy or that everyone likes you. In particular, evaluate statistical evaluations over more than one course or semester -- what is consistent across several courses? Are there low scores that recur across different courses? If so, consider the reasons and take steps to actively improve in those areas.

Evaluate yourself—most research supports the view that your honest analysis of your own teaching generally coincides with outside observers' evaluations. In order to stimulate your thinking on the subject, fill out a typical student evaluation form as though you were a student in your classroom.

Ask someone else to evaluate your teaching—choose someone who is experienced enough to be able to help you as well as candid enough to be honest and supportive of your efforts to improve. Sit down together and discussion your strengths and limitations. Ask for specific suggestions for improvement.

Videotape yourself—you will want to videotape one or several class periods, wait several days, and then when you have established some distance from the class periods, review the tapes and judge for yourself what they reveal. Caution: We tend to focus on physical characteristics and ignore content variables when we view videotapes. You might use the list of questions included at the end of this section to guide your thinking.

Practice new teaching techniques—force yourself to try a new approach to teaching. If you have never used discussion in your class, read about the techniques, plan a good set of stimulating questions, and experiment with classroom discussion. You may need several experiences with the new technique before it becomes comfortable for you, so don't be impatient if it does not work well immediately. Keep experimenting.

Develop a Teaching Portfolio—since much of the useful information about your teaching is unique to your discipline and even to your approach to your classes, it may be most useful to develop an individual teaching portfolio that captures the special nature of your teaching. Most portfolios are descriptive and developmental. They engage the instructor in reflective assessment. There are many models to follow in preparing a teaching portfolio, but one, in particular, provides a comprehensive approach: Laurie Richlin and Brenda Manning, Improving A College/University Teaching Evaluation System (Pittsburgh, PA: Alliance Publishers, 1995). Another edited collection that would be useful to examine is Kathleen Blake Yancey and Irwin Weiser, Eds., Situating Portfolios: Four Perspectives (Logan, UT: Utah State University Press, 1997).

Read about teaching—there are several excellent books on the subject of teaching as well as general education journals and communication journals devoted to instructional innovation and development. State, regional, and national conventions also frequently sponsor programs presenting teaching strategies and research. See reference section below on Teaching Resources.

J. References

1.   Communication Anxiety

Bippus, Amy D. and John A. Daly, "What Do People Think Causes Stage Fright?: Naïve Attributions about the Reasons for Public Speaking Anxiety," Communication Education 48 (1999): 63-72

Kougl, Kathleen M. "Dealing with Quiet Students in the Basic College Speech Course." Communication Education 29 (1980): 234-238.

McCroskey, James C. "Classroom Consequences of Communication Apprehension." Communication Education 26 (1977): 27-33.

McCroskey, James C. "The Implementation of a Large-Scale Program of Systematic Desensitization for Communication Apprehension." Speech Teacher 21 (1972): 255-264.

McCroskey, James C. "Oral Communication Apprehension: A Summary of Recent Theory and Research." Human Communication Research 4 (1977): 78-96.

Robinson, Thomas E. "Communication Apprehension and the Basic Public Speaking Course: A National Survey of In-Class Treatment Techniques," Communication Education 46 (1997): 188-197.

2.   Critical Thinking

Brookfield, Stephen D. Becoming a Critically Reflective Teacher. Jossey-Bass Publishers, 1995.

Browne, M. Neil and Stuart M. Kelley, Asking the right questions : a guide to critical thinking. 6th ed Imprint. Upper Saddle River, N.J. : Prentice Hall, 2001.

Chance, Paul. "Master of Mastery: Benjamin S. Bloom." Psychology Today 21 (1987): 43-46.

Little, Linda and Ingrid A. Greenberg, <u>Problem Solving : Critical Thinking and Communication Skills</u>. New York: Addison-Wesley, 1991

Stratton, Jon. <u>Critical thinking for college students</u>. Lanham, Md.: Rowman & Littlefield, 1999.

3.   <u>Teaching and Learning Styles</u>.

Brockbank, Anne and Ian McGill, <u>Facilitating Reflective Learning in Higher Education</u>. Open University Press, 1998.

Dunn, Rita Stafford and Kenneth J. Dunn, <u>The Complete Guide to the Learning Styles Inservice System</u>. Boston: Allyn & Bacon, 1999.

Gardner, Howard. "Beyond the IQ: Education and human development." <u>National Forum</u> 68 (1988): 4-7.

Grasha, Anthony. <u>Teaching with Style</u>. Pittsburgh, PA: Alliance Publishers, 1996.

Jalongo, Mary Renk, Meghan Mahoney Tweist, and Gail J. Gerlach, <u>The College Learner: Reading, Studying, and Attaining Academic Success</u>. Prentice Hall, 1998.

Johnson, David W. and Roger T. Johnson, <u>Learning Together and Alone: Cooperative, Competitive, and Individualistic Learning</u>. Boston: Allyn & Bacon, 1999.

McKerrow, Raymie E. "Rhetoric and the Construction of a Deliberative Community."<u>Southern Communication Journal</u> 63 (1998): 350-356.

Sternberg, R. J. "Beyond IQ Testing." <u>National Forum</u> 68 (1988): 8-11.

4.   <u>Teaching Resources</u>

Brown, Sallie A. and Douglas E. Miller. <u>The Active Learner : Successful Study Strategies</u>. 3rd Ed., Los Angeles, Calif.: Roxbury, 2001.

Buehl, Doug. <u>Classroom Strategies for Interactive Learning</u>. 2nd Ed., Newark, Del.: International Reading Association, 2001.

Coffey, Amanda, and Sara Delamont. <u>Feminism and the Classroom Teacher: Research, Praxis, and Pedagogy</u>. London ; New York: Routledge/Falmer, 2000.

Cooper, Pamela J. <u>Speech Communication for the Classroom Teacher</u>, 2nd ed., Dubuque, IA: Gorsuch Scarisbrick, 1984.

Evans, Terry and Daryl Nation. (Eds). <u>Changing University Teaching : Reflections on Creating Educational Technologies</u>. Sterling, VA : Stylus Pub., 2000

Grasha, Anthony. <u>Teaching with Style</u>. Pittsburgh: Alliance Publishers, 1996.

Jensen, Karla Kay and Vinnie Harris, "The Public Speaking Portfolio." <u>Communication Education</u> 48 (1999): 211-27.

Kumar, Amitava. (Ed.). <u>Class Issues: Pedagogy, Cultural Studies, and the Public Sphere</u>. New York : New York University Press, 1997.

Lantis, Jeffrey S., Lynn M. Kuzma and John Boehrer. (Eds.). <u>The New International Studies Classroom: Active Teaching, Active Learning</u>. Boulder, Colo.: Lynne Rienner, 2000.

Richlin, Laurie, and Brenda Manning. <u>Improving A College/University Teaching Evaluation System</u>. Pittsburgh, PA: Alliance Publishers, 1995.

Shapiro, H. S. And David E. Purpel. (Eds). Critical Social Issues in American Education: Transformation in a Postmodern World. 2nd ed. Mahwah, N.J. : L. Erlbaum Associates, 1998.

Stevens, Sunnye R., "How to go into the Lion's Den and Bring Out a Kitty Cat: First Day Strategies for Graduate Teaching Assistants." Communication Teacher 14 (2000):10-12.

The Best of Works4Me: Winning Tips from Classroom Teachers. Washington, D.C.: NEA Professional Library, National Education Association, 2000.

Yancey, Kathleen Blake, and Irwin Weiser. (Eds.). Situating Portfolios: Four Perspectives. Logan, UT: Utah State University Press, 1997.

5.   Assessment

Aitken, Joan and Michael Neer. "A Faculty Program of Assessment for a College Level Competency-Based Communication Core Curriculum." Communication Education 41 (1992): 270-286.

Backlund, P. Ellen Hay, S. Harper, and D. Williams. "Assessing the Outcomes of College: Implications for Speech Communication." Association for Communication Administration Bulletin 72 (1990): 7-10.

Goulden, Nancy. "Theory and Vocabulary for Communication Assessments." Communication Education 41 (1992): 258-269.

Gschwend, Laura, "Every Student Deserves an Assessment Tool that Teaches." Communication Teacher 14 (2000):1-5

GUIDELINES FOR ASSESSING A VIDEOTAPE OF YOUR TEACHING

Videotape yourself teaching one or more classes. Allow several days to pass, then view the videotape. As you reflect on what you've seen, answer the following questions:

1.   *Did you start and end your class on time?*
2.   *Did you permit questions before and after class began?*
3.   *Did students seem to feel comfortable asking questions during class?*
4.   *Did you know your students' names?*
5.   *Did you start the class with a preview or forecast?*
6.   *Did you summarize the class session and reach closure at the end of the class period?*
7.   *Did you outline the key concepts covered during the class?*
8.   *Was it easy for students to take notes on important ideas?*
9.   *Did you bring in information, ideas, or exercises beyond those included in the textbook?*
10.   *Did you tie information to student assignments?*
11.   *During discussion, did you:*
      a.   *Reward student responses to questions?*
      b.   *Use positive nonverbal reinforcement?*
      c.   *Ask a variety of questions beyond simple regurgitation questions?*
      d.   *Allow adequate time for students to develop their answers?*
      e.   *Include more than a few students in the discussion?*
      f.   *Encourage students to add to the discussion by asking questions of their own?*
      g.   *Guide the discussion as it evolved?*
      h.   *Summarize the key ideas generated during the discussion?*
12.   *Did you maintain the attention of students during the class?*
13.   *Did you notice any distracting mannerisms in your presentation of class material?*
14.   *Did you seem comfortable but animated?*
15.   *Did you use class time efficiently?*
16.   *During class, did you:*
      a.   *Include current events?*
      b.   *Use audiovisual materials?*
      c.   *Record important concepts on the chalkboard?*
      d.   *Clarify ideas with examples or illustrations?*
      e.   *Provide opportunities for active learning on the part of students (as opposed to serving up ideas only via lecture/discussion)?*
17.   *What is your primary strength as an instructor?*
18.   *What improvements have you noticed in your teaching since the last term?*
19.   *What limitations did you notice in your teaching?*
20.   *List two or three goals for improvement in your teaching.*

SECTION II: INSTRUCTIONAL STRATEGIES AND MATERIALS

This section is provided to give you ideas about how to teach the individual chapters from the textbook. By no means an exhaustive account of the teaching strategies that can be employed, it serves, hopefully, a heuristic function. The suggestions here may serve as springboards for more creative ways to address the content of the textbook.

For each chapter from the textbook, the main concepts are summarized. This summary is followed by general discussion questions and more advanced questions to stimulate critical thinking. You can use these questions as you plan your classroom discussions or lectures. These questions are followed by supplemental materials in the form of application exercises, impromptu speaking activities, selected additional resources, and student participation forms. These supplemental materials can be used to expand your classroom activities.

The application exercises attempt to reinforce chapter concepts through practical application or drill. Impromptu speaking activities incorporate the chapter concepts with performance aimed at improving the skills of delivery as well as preparing students to make effective rhetorical choices.

Additional resources include articles, books, or other materials which may provide additional classroom activities or further elaboration of the concepts stressed in the chapters. Finally, several student participation forms are attached. These forms are ready for duplication or adaptation for your classroom.

For additional teaching ideas, use the activities following each of the chapters in the textbook to stimulate student participation and further investigation of the textbook content.

CHAPTER 1.   THE ACADEMIC STUDY OF PUBLIC SPEAKING

CHAPTER CONTENT

Studying Public Speaking in Higher Education
    The Need for Speech Training
    Ways to Learn More about Public Speaking
The Functions of Public Speaking in Society
    Orality in Social-Political Life
    Public Speaking and Decision Making in a Multicultural Society
    Achieving Personal and Collective Goals through Public Talk
The Centrality of Ethics in Public Communication
    Ethos in the Western World
    The Moral Bases of Public Decision Making
    How to Enhance your Credibility as a Public Speaker
Skills and Competencies Needed for Successful Speechmaking
    Integrity
    Knowledge
    Rhetorical Sensitivity
    Oral Skills
    Self-Confidence
Public Speaking as a Liberal Art
    How to Manage Your Fear of Public Speaking
    Freeing Yourself
    Making a Free Society Work
Chapter Summary
Key Terms
Assessment Activities
References

Discussion Questions

1.   Is there a relationship between expertise in speaking and career advancement?
2.   What is the relationship between speech training and a liberal education?
3.   Why is speech training important in a diverse culture?
4.   What important functions do public speeches perform for a society? Provide several examples of each.
5.   What does it mean to speak ethically?
6.   What opportunities have you had to speak in public? What future opportunities will you probably have to use public communication skills?
7.   What four key elements must every speaker consider in the speaking situation?
8.   How can you begin to achieve confidence as a public speaker?

Questions to Stimulate Critical Thinking

1.   What roles do you see yourself playing in our contemporary culture and how does that role relate to training in public communication?
2.   With respect to ethics and "moral frames" as noted in this chapter, what are the most common moral frames in which you will find yourself speaking?
3.   As a classroom speaker, how can you be rhetorically sensitive?
4.   How can a speaker improve self-image if s/he lacks confidence in speaking?
5.   Is it ethical for an individual with an unscrupulous message to project themselves as highly credible?
6.   Identify several people in public life who you consider to be "principled speakers." What do they have in common that accounts for their reputation as ethical communicators?
7.   Do you believe that speaking in public, as suggested in the text, will be a "freeing act?" Why or why not?

Application Exercises

Chapter-Based Exercises [in each case, also see the Assessment Activities at the end of each chapter]

1. Studying Public Speaking
   A. Objective: To identify reasons for the study of public speaking in higher education.
   B. Procedure: Based on their reading, ask students to identify the reasons (may include reasons not covered in text):
)   To gain knowledge as consumers
   2)   To obtain skills relevant to a liberal education
   3)   To maximize personal and collective goals
   4)   To be aware of the impact of a diverse culture on how we communicate
   5.   To understand the need for sensitivity as a communicator.
   C. Discussion: Who are some of the student's role models as public communicators? What kind of role do they see these people playing in social and political life, and to what extent is their success dependent on their skill as public speakers?

2. Recognizing Diversity
   A. Objective: To highlight the importance of multiple perspectives among prominent public speakers.
   B. Procedure: Ask each student to identify a contemporary public speaker who represents diversity in this society. If they have difficulty suggesting names other than Jesse Jackson and Colin Powell ask why it is harder to name people of color as major public figures/spokepersons?
   C. Discussion: In naming a variety of spokespersons, what viewpoint does each speaker represent and how does that contribute to the public discussion of issues? If struggling to name persons of color, what does this say about society's acceptance of diversity? What are the most effective ways to voice diverse opinions in public? How do widely-held public opinions come to be endorsed by a majority of people? [Note: we will return to this central concern in Chapter 4 in a more detailed discussion of teaching objectives/strategies]

3. Skills and Competencies
    A. Objective: To encourage an initial appraisal of skill development at this stage.
    B. Procedure: After a short discussion of the skills and competencies needed for successful speaking, divide a chalkboard into four columns and head each of the columns with one of the following: Integrity, Knowledge, Rhetorical Sensitivity, Oral Skills. If not already asked (see C. above) ask students to think of public speakers or prominent public figures who exemplify these skills and competencies. If already asked, pursue in more depth in relation to these skills. Which skills do the students feel are their weakest?
    C. Discussion: Do some public speakers fall into more than one category? Ensuing discussion might concentrate on the effectiveness of speakers and the variety of skills they possess.

4. Community Speaker Interview
    A. Objective: To develop an appreciation for the role of public speaking in the local community.
    B. Procedure: Ask each student to interview a person whose role in the community requires public speaking. You might suggest individuals such as religious leaders, community activists, local political figures, charity workers, business people, and others. Review the requirements of good interview technique. You may use the Interview Form included at the end of this chapter.
    C. Discussion: How important is skilled public speaking for the person you interviewed? In what contexts does he/she use public speaking? How do they prepare to speak in public? How do they deal with communication anxiety? You may want to compare answers to the questions on the Interview Form.

5. Additional Exercises: Students should be asked to complete the Personal Data Sheet and Assessing Your Personal Speaking Goals following this section. Students' answers to the Communication Quiz can be discussed in small groups or as a class. You may also wish to review the Criteria for Grading with your students. In addition, a Self-Assessment form is included to use with your early speaking assignments.

Impromptu Speaking Activities

1. Get Acquainted Exercise
    A. Objective: To minimize student apprehension during the initial class meetings.
    B. Procedure: Form a circle of chairs or another informal physical setting. The instructor should begin by telling everyone his/her name then saying a few things about himself/herself. Each member of the class should do the same, attempting to name each of the previous speakers before giving his/her name and something about himself/herself. The discussion following this activity might focus on how the attempt to recall names is affected by apprehension or how this group will function as an audience during the term.

2. Variations on a Theme
    A. Objective: To introduce students to their classmates and help them remember each others' names.
    B. Procedure: Form a circle of chairs and ask each student to give everyone his/her name and identify their major. After everyone has spoken, ask them to give their names again, but this time explain why they chose their major. After this round, ask students

to repeat their names and explain how communication could be important in their major or career.

3. Dyad Exercise

A. Objective: To allow students to get acquainted with their classmates on a one-to-one basis.

B. Procedure: Assign pairs or ask that each student find a partner. Give students a limited time to talk with their partner. After 2-3 minutes, signal students to switch partners and begin a new conversation. Repeat as time permits or until most of the class has interacted. The conversation might focus on demographics such as: Where are you from? What is your major? What is your favorite pastime? Or questions might directly relate to chapter readings/public communication such as: Who would you say is a rhetorically sensitive public communicator? What constitutes an ethical communicator? The Ice Breaker form at the end of this chapter also provides questions to begin the conversation.

4. Interview Exercise

A. Objective: To get students on their feet for their first impromptu speech while getting them acquainted with their classmates and future audience members.

B. Procedure: Assign pairs or allow students to chose partners, preferably someone they don't already know. Allow students 15-20 minutes to "interview" each other or give them the remainder of the class period. During the following class period ask students to volunteer or call on them to introduce their partner in a short, informal impromptu speech. The apprehension level in this first impromptu can be lessened
if a circle is formed and students are allowed to sit while addressing the group. You may duplicate and distribute the Ice Breaker questions following this chapter to get your students started.

5. Who Am I?

A. Objective: To allow students to explore their heritage and share it with class members.

B. Procedure: Ask each student to investigate their lineage. They should note origins of their parents and grandparents as well as traditions important in their family. Place students in groups of 3 or 4 to share their backgrounds. Follow up this exercise with a discussion of audience analysis and adaptation.

6. Round Robin Impromptu

A. Objective: To allow the students to experience answering questions.

B. Procedure: Have a student ask another in the same row a question [indicate that the questions should be easy ones to answer, as in why they selected their major, what their home town is like, etc.]. When that student finishes answering the question, have him or her ask the next person and so on through the class . . . the last person to speak asks the first person who started the process. Ask them to speak for one to two minutes.

Additional Resources

Berko, Roy. "Getting to Know You and Talking About It." <u>Speech Communication</u>
    <u>Teacher</u> 7 (1993): 5-6.
Curtis, Dan B., Jerry L. Winsor, and Ronald D. Stephens, "National Preferences in Business and
    Communication Education." <u>Communication Education</u> 38 (1989): 6-14.
Ford, Wendy Zabava and Andrew Wolvin. "The Differential Impact of a Basic Communication
    Course on Perceived Communication Competencies in Class, Work, and Social
    Contexts." <u>Communication Education</u> 42 (1993): 215-223.
Isaacson, Zelda. "Paradoxical Intention: A Strategy to Alleviate the Anxiety Associated with
    Public Speaking." <u>Speech Communication Teacher</u> 7 (1993): 13-14.
Powell, Kimberly. "Increasing Appreciation for Diversity Through the Group Culture Speech."
    <u>Speech Communication Teacher</u> 10 (1996): 3-4.
West, Richard. "Can We Talk? Using the Personal Reference Inventory as an Ice Breaker."
    <u>Speech Communication Teacher</u> 7 (1993): 12-13.

Answers to Communication Quiz (See p. 46)
    1 - T, 2 - T, 3 - F, 4 - T, 5 - F, 6 - F, 7 - F, 8 - F, 9 - F, 10 - T

INTERVIEW FORM

1. How important is being perceived as a skilled public speaking to you?

2. What is your primary strength as a public speaker?

3. How did you learn to speak in public and as you learned, how did you polish your speaking skills?

4. In what contexts do you use public speaking?

5. How do you prepare to speak in public?

6. Do you experience anxiety about speaking in public? How do you deal with it?

7. How do you adapt to your audience as you prepare your speeches? What factors do you take into consideration as you prepare?

8. What is the most difficult public speaking situation you have encountered? How did you adapt to it?

9. What advice would you give someone who is just learning to speak in public?

[Express your appreciation for the interviewee's time and cooperation.]

PERSONAL DATA SHEET

Name:_____Campus Phone: _____ Email: _____

Year: Fr__ So ___Jr ___Sr ___ Major: _____

Career or Future Goals:

Hobbies:

If you have had previous speech experience or training, please describe when, where, and of what type:

Please rank your top <u>four</u> goals in order of priority:

___ To improve my voice and articulation

___ To become more fluent

___ To gain confidence and poise

___ To learn to deliver a speech effectively

___ To learn about communication theories

___ To organize my ideas logically

___ To become a better listener

___ To learn to evaluate the speaking of others

___ To learn to influence listeners more effectively

___ To overcome my reluctance to speak up in groups of people

___ To prepare for a career requiring an ability to speak in public

Do you feel you have any specific concerns or needs which may relate to this course?

Please add any comments you think would help your instructor understand you and your needs better:

ASSESSING YOUR PERSONAL SPEAKING GOALS

Circle the appropriate number for each of the follow statements. Then, consider your strengths and weaknesses in speaking. Determine which items you will work on for the course.

1 = strongly disagree 2 = disagree 3 = neutral 4 = agree 5 = strongly agree

1. 1 2 3 4 5 I feel comfortable speaking with people in conversations.
2. 1 2 3 4 5 I am a good listener.
3. 1 2 3 4 5 I project a positive self-image.
4. 1 2 3 4 5 I have often prepared and presented speeches.
5. 1 2 3 4 5 I can usually find topics to talk about.
6. 1 2 3 4 5 I consider other people's points of view.
7. 1 2 3 4 5 I am usually clear and organized when I present my ideas.
8. 1 2 3 4 5 I am confident and relaxed when I speak to others.
9. 1 2 3 4 5 I often use supporting material to back up my ideas.
10. 1 2 3 4 5 I can capture and hold people's attention when I talk.
11. 1 2 3 4 5 I choose words that suit my listeners and my topic.
12. 1 2 3 4 5 I use natural gestures when speaking.
13. 1 2 3 4 5 I look at people when I talk to them.
14. 1 2 3 4 5 I can use visual aids effectively.
15. 1 2 3 4 5 I can present information so it is easy to understand.
16. 1 2 3 4 5 I can construct logical and effective arguments.
17. 1 2 3 4 5 I am often successful at convincing people to see my point of view.
18. 1 2 3 4 5 I participate in classroom discussions.
19. 1 2 3 4 5 I feel comfortable asking questions in class.
20. 1 2 3 4 5 I can participate effectively in small group discussions.

CRITERIA FOR GRADING

I.   An average (C) speech meets the following standards:
       A.   Conforms to speaking assignment
       B.   Conforms reasonably to the time limits
       C.   Exhibits sound organization--a clear purpose adequately supported by main ideas that are easily identified
       D.   Develops an intellectually sound, worthwhile topic with adequate and dependable supporting materials
       E.   Fulfills any special requirements of the assignment, such as, use of three types of supporting material
       F.   Exhibits reasonable directness and conversationality in delivery
       G.   Is correct in grammar, pronunciation, and articulation
       H.   Is presented on the assigned date

II.   The above average (B) speech meets the preceding requirements and also:
       A.   Challenges the audience to think or arouses in listeners a depth of response
       B.   Demonstrates skills in winning understanding of unusually difficult concepts or processes; or in winning agreement from auditors initially inclined to disagree with the speaker's purpose
       C.   Establishes genuine rapport and interaction with listeners through content and delivery
       D.   Exhibits well developed and clearly communicated organizational substructure as well as transitions and internal previews and summaries
       E.   Reveals outside supporting materials which are considered exceptionally relevant and authoritative on the topic

III.   The superior (A) speech not only meets the previous standards, but also:
       A.   Contributes exceptional individual thinking and research on the speech topic
       B.   Achieves the variety and flexibility of mood and manner demanded by the subject matter and by the speaker-audience interaction
       C.   Achieves a demonstrable progression from the initial attitudes held by the audience toward a final resolution of ideas
       D.   Illustrates skillful mastery of internal transitions and of presentation of the speaker's ideas

IV.   Below average speeches (D or F) are deficient in some or several of the factors required for an average speech

NOTE: Any speech presented after the date assigned or read from notes will not receive above a C grade.

ICE BREAKER

<u>Instructions</u>: Your instructor will pair you with another person in the class. Make sure that you do not know this person. You will be given time to get to know each other by asking questions. At the end of your conversation, you will be asked to introduce your partner to the rest of the class. You will want to tell the class something to help them remember the person. The following questions will get you started, but you need to go beyond them:

1.   Name: _____

2.   Age: _____

3.   Major: _____

4.   What helped you decide on your major?

5.   Favorite books? TV shows? movies? magazines? animals?

6.   Hobbies?

7.   Sports? favorite teams?

8.   Jobs held?

9.   Places visited?

10.   Special talents?

11.   Embarrassing experiences?

12.   Heroes?

13.   Exciting experiences?

14.   Things that bore you?

15.   Why did you choose this school?

SELF-ASSESSMENT

Prepare this evaluation of your first speech and hand it to your instructor the class period following the speech:

1.   How well do you think you expressed your main ideas?

2.   What were your main strengths in delivery the speech?

3.   What were your main weaknesses in delivery?

4.   What are you going to do to overcome these weaknesses in the next oral assignment? Be specific.

5.   Recognizing the fact that performance anxiety is normal during speaking, what were you able to do to channel this anxiety productively? What symptoms of this anxiety will you expect in your next speech? How will you plan to channel those effectively?

COMMUNICATION QUIZ

<u>Directions</u>: Circle T (True) or F (False) for each of the following statements.

T F 1. There is a strong social imperative that persons be capable of expressing their ideas in public settings.

T F 2. Knowledge of public communication is the best defense against its misuse.

T F 3. Public speaking has little to do with the formation of communities.

T F 4. Communication may be used to create unity in the midst of diversity.

T F 5. The debate over political correctness is unrelated to the study of communication.

T F 6. A rhetorically sensitive speaker is one who is primarily sensitive to her/his own needs

T F 7. Trait apprehension refers to the anxiety you feel in specific communication situations.

T F 8. The principled speaker is one who knows what is best for audiences, and hence gives them less responsibility for making decisions.

T F 9. A confident speaker has no anxiety about speaking in public.

T F 10. The principled speaker is one who focuses on the audience's expectations.

CHAPTER 2.   GETTING STARTED: BASIC TIPS FOR SPEECH PREPARATION AND DELIVERY

CHAPTER CONTENT

Selecting the Subject
Narrowing the Subject
     How to Narrow a Topic: An Illustration
Determining the Purposes
     General Purposes
     Specific Purposes
     Central Idea or Claim
     Creating the Title
     Strategic Considerations
Analyzing the Audience and the Occasion
Gathering the Speech Materials
Outlining the Speech
Practicing Aloud
     Ethical Moments: Ethics and Public Speaking
Delivering Your Speech Confidently
     Selecting the Method of Presentation
     Communicating Self Confidence
Learning to Evaluate Speeches
Assessing a Sample Speech: "Clearing the Air about Cigars," Dena Craig
Chapter Summary
Key Terms
Assessment Activities
References

Discussion Questions

1.   What does it mean to have a rhetorical frame of mind?
2.   What are the essential steps in preparing to speak?
3.   Provide some guidelines to help a speaker select a subject that's appropriate to the rhetorical situation.
4.   How do you determine if your speech topic will interest your listeners?
5.   How does the occasion influence your selection of a speech topic?

6.   Why should you narrow the speech topic? How do you know if the speech topic needs to be narrowed?

7.   What three primary considerations will help you narrow your speech topic?

8.   What is the general purpose of a speech?

9.   What are the differences among speeches to inform, to persuade, to actuate, and to entertain?

10.   What is the difference between the general purpose and the specific purpose of the speech?

11.   Why would one distinguish between a central idea and claim?

12.   Why would one distinguish between "persuade" and "actuate" as general purposes?

13.   What guidelines will help you select your speech title?

14.   What strategic considerations will determine your actual decisions as you plan your speech?

15.   What kinds of information should you gather as you analyze your speech audience?

16.   Where can you discover material to develop your speech?

17.   Why should you outline your speech?

18.   How should you practice your speech before it is given?

19.   What are the four methods of presenting a speech? Which is most appropriate for classroom speaking?

20.   How can you communicate self-confidence while speaking?

21.   What are important considerations to make while you are evaluating the speeches of others?

Questions to Stimulate Critical Thinking

1.   Should your interests, your audience's needs and the demands of the occasion be equally weighted as you prepare your speech? Discuss this question using actual instances to support your point of view.

2.   Under what conditions should the speaker's option to choose the speech topic be restricted?

3.   How do audience, occasion, and speech topic interact? Use a specific example to explain the process.

4.   Some communication scholars argue that communication is never purely neutral or just for your information. Do you agree? Why or why not?

5.   Does the relationship between the speaker and audience change as the general purpose of the speech changes?

6.   Why is it sound advice to practice your speech aloud?

7.   Identify several examples of each kind of general speech purpose. Explain the differences among them.

8.   Is it ever ethical for a speaker to hide the ultimate aim of a speech from the audience?

9.   Discuss the relationship between the method of speech presentation and the occasion.

10.   How could a speaker use a speech title to mislead the audience? Is this ethical?

Application Exercises

1. Identifying the Steps in Speech Preparation

A. Objective: To facilitate recognition of the essential steps in speech preparation.

B. Procedure: After reading a sample speech provided in the text, ask students to reconstruct the steps the speaker probably went through before the final speech was written. You might, for example, discuss what broader subject this speech was developed from, what audience/occasion the speech was designed for, etc.

C. Discussion: Focus on the similarity in the steps a speaker must take in preparing a speech despite frequently very different speeches.

2. Determining Speaking Purposes

A. Objective: To encourage students to think of the purpose of public communication in varied situations.

B. Procedure: Provide situations such as the following and ask students as a class or in groups to identify a private, public, short-term, and long-term purpose for each speaker:

1) A U.S. president addressing the nation on the economy during an election year

2) A classroom instructor reviewing material over which a test is scheduled

3) A labor negotiator calling together representatives of labor and management

4) A student telephoning his/her parents for money

C. Discussion: In each of these situations alter one or another of the variables and determine if the purposes of the communication are affected.

3. Phrasing the Central Idea/Claim

A. Objective: To illustrate to students how vital language intensity is in transmitting the speaker's objectives.

B. Procedure: Ask students for sample central ideas or claims for speeches or provide some prepared examples. Record each on a chalkboard, leaving space below it. Ask students to re-phrase each example in increasingly intense language.

C. Discussion: Speculate on the speaker's intentions in each of these versions of the central idea or claim. Also identify the potential audiences for each.

4. Narrowing the Speech Topic

A. Objective: To provide the student practice in selecting and narrowing the speech topic.

B. Procedure: Assign groups or work with the class as a whole. Using brainstorming techniques, ask for ideas for speeches. Write each general idea on the board, then when 10-15 ideas have been recorded, proceed to narrow each to several specific speech topics.

C. Discussion: Probe the differences between the general topic area and the specific topic for the speech. Recognize that one general topic might yield several very different narrowed speech topics.

5. Determining Speech Purposes

A. Objective: To provide practice in determining general and specific speaking purposes.

B. Procedure: Provide students with copies of the worksheet included at the end of this chapter. Ask them to complete the worksheet, filling in their general purpose, specific purpose, and speech title for each of the five topics. Compare the results.

C. Discussion: What general purposes did you determine for each of the topics? How does the general purpose affect the specific purpose? Does your speech title reflect your general and specific purpose? What is the function of the speech title?

6. Identifying the Method of Presentation

A. Objective: To encourage students to choose the most appropriate method of presentation before they speak.

B. Procedure: Brainstorm and list public speaking situations on the chalkboard. Then, determine which method of presentation would be best for each public speaking situation.

C. Discussion: Explain why the method of presentation chosen is best for each situation. What are the advantages of each method of presentation? What are the limitations of each? What factors are important to consider when choosing the method of presentation?

7. Additional Applications: At this point, you may wish to include a discussion of communication apprehension. You may also assign the work sheets for brainstorming, planning the speech, and the narrative speech assignment found at the end of this chapter.

Impromptu Speaking Activities

1. Proverbs and Maxims
   A. Objective: To focus attention on communicating a single central idea or thesis.
   B. Procedure: Provide students with common proverbs (for example, "A stitch in time saves nine"). Ask them to interpret the proverb in an impromptu speech.

2. Your Hometown
   A. Objective: To provide students an opportunity to practice using forecasting in a simple speech on a topic which is familiar to them.
   B. Procedure: Ask students to think of 2 or 3 things that make their hometown an attractive place to visit. Then, after reinforcing the importance of forecasting in a speech or providing an example of forecasting, ask students to relate the features of their hometown which make it an interesting place to visit. Make sure that they use a forecast in the beginning of this impromptu speech.

3. Name That Speech
   A. Objective: To stimulate students to think about what a title communicates about the content of a speech.
   B. Procedure: Have students make up fictitious titles; using a round-robin approach, have one student present a title, and ask another student to either make up a short speech to fit the title or discuss what the title probably means. This can also assist in improving impromptu speaking skills.

4. Group Speech
   A. Objective: To encourage students to consider the elements that influence the choice of speech subject and purpose.
   B. Procedure: Divide the class into small groups of five. Write the five factors influencing the choice of speech subject and purpose on the chalkboard. Ask each group to decide on a speech situation other than a classroom speech and choose a subject for that situation. Then, ask each member of the group to briefly discuss one of the five factors which influenced the choice of the speech subject and purpose.

5. Confidence Builders
   A. Objective: To develop students' confidence in speaking by providing brief opportunities for them to address the class.
   B. Procedure: During the first few days of the term, ask each student to give a 10 to 15 second speech at the beginning of class.   Their comments can be used to introduce the lecture topic for the class period. You might use the following:

1) List a quality, characteristic, or behavior that you like. For example: "I like an autonomous individual, someone who has an opinion and sticks by it, even though their opinion makes them unpopular."

2) Describe the target audience for a television advertisement. Use a characteristic of audiences mentioned in the textbook. For example: "The <u>age</u> of the audience is an important characteristic in Levi's commercials. These ads are targeted toward young college students."

3) Tell the class a fact. For example: "Did you know that according to (cite the source) many guys in their twenties are marrying older women because there is a shortage of eligible women in their own age group?"

4) Deliver a toast to anyone of your choice. For example: "I would like to propose a toast to my best friend (say their name) because she has always been there to listen and support me."

5) Recite a line or phrase from prose or poetry that rhymes, uses a metaphor, simile or some other literary device. Make sure to cite the author's name.

(This exercise was used with the permission of Professor Carl Thameling, Miami University-Hamilton.)

Additional Resources

Ayres, Joe and Debbie Ayres Sonandré, "Speech Criticism and Group Presentations," <u>Speech Communication Teacher</u> 13 (Fall 1999): 14-15.

Ayres, Joe, <u>Speech Sampler: Speeches and Analyses</u>. Ruston:WA: Communication Ventures, 1997.

Carlson, Robert E. and Deborah Smith-Howell, "Classroom Public Speaking Assessment: Reliability and Validity of Selected Evaluation Instruments." <u>Communication Education</u> 44 (1995): 87-97.

Menzel, K. and Loris Carrell. "The Relationship Between Preparation and Performance in Public Speaking." <u>Communication Education</u> 43 (1994): 17-26.

Woodside, Daria. "Choosing Topics for Speeches." <u>Speech Communication Teacher</u> 7 (1992): 1-2.

Public Speaking Portfolios

One approach to use as the course begins is to have students create their own portfolios. The requirements for portfolio creation are as varied as the circumstances may warrant. Your objective may be to engage students in a more consistent appraisal of their own performance, both in classroom speeches and on exams. If so, this approach is an excellent way to accomplish your goal.

What follows is borrowed in part from a recent article by Karla Kay Jensen and Vinnie Harris (The Public Speaking Portfolio, Communication Education 48 (1999): 211-227.

Portfolio Components:

Journal writing: you can ask students to write daily or following each class session. The goal of journal writing is to chronicle events as they occur: what questions do students have as they read, listen to lecture or participate in discussion? What do they agree or disagree with? One constant may be the role of ethics: what are the personal ethics of the students, and how are these challenged or refined during the course? Students also can seek to make connections from one class period to the next – or across early and later class periods. What is the value of the connections in preparing them to speak later in the quarter or semester?

Speech Process Log: This activity chronicles the speech history from initial preparation to reflection on the presentation. It may include the outline – comments on what information was easy or hard to obtain. The reflection section may examine the organizational strategy, comment on delivery problems, or focus on things to do better the next time. As part of this log, classroom comments as well as instructor comments should be included. The section may also include other artifacts related to topics.

Video-Taped Performances: If the technology is available, students should have a single video-tape that contains their performances.

Critical Evaluations: If critical responses to public speeches are included as part of the course requirements, the portfolio could contain copies of written evaluations produced by the student. Students might also be asked, depending on timing, to critically reflect on the instructor's evaluation of their written work: what do they agree with or disagree with, and what might they do differently in a future analysis?

DETERMINING SPEAKING PURPOSES

Directions: For each of the topics listed below, determine a general and specific speech purposes and speech title.

1.   Sports

      General purpose:

      Specific purpose:

      Speech title:

2.   Politics

      General purpose:

      Specific purpose:

      Speech title:

3.   Poverty

      General purpose:

      Specific purpose:

      Speech title:

4.   Parenthood

      General purpose:

      Specific purpose:

      Speech title:

BRAINSTORMING

Acquaint yourself with the fundamental guidelines for brainstorming:

1.   Appoint a recorder.
2.   Jot down every idea/comment which is made.
3.   Do not editorialize/evaluate/elaborate on ideas. Just state them as quickly and concisely as possible.
4.   Don't overlook the obvious. It may trigger an idea from someone else.
5.   Don't be afraid to repeat ideas in different wording. This may lead to a different interpretation or way of thinking.
6.   Only when contributions have stopped should you go back and begin to sort out and evaluate the list of ideas.

To learn brainstorming, you must practice it. Form groups or act as a committee of the whole and practice this technique on the following problems:

1.   How can an egg be packaged so that it will not break when dropped from the top of a 20-foot ladder?

2.   What adjustments would our society have to make if there were three sexes instead of two?

3.   How do you talk to aliens who have just landed if they don't speak any known human language?

4.   How can you divide up the ocean's resources for individual nation's economic development?

5.   If you had a million dollars to spend on academic improvement, how would you allocate the money?

TOPIC SELECTION CHECKLIST

As you consider topics for your speech assignments, use this checklist to determine if this is an appropriate topic.

1. Will this topic meet the purpose of the speech assignment?

2. How much do you currently know about this topic?

3. Is material readily available in your library or can you find resource persons for interviews?

4. How do you think your listeners will respond to this topic?

5. How do you think your instructor will respond to this topic?

6. Is this topic related to something you are currently interested in?

7. Can the topic be narrowed to a single central point?

8. If you divided this topic into two or three smaller topic areas, what would they be? Would these be more appropriate for your time constraints?

9. What visual aids are available to use on this topic?

10. Am I a credible speaker on this topic?

11. Would a speech on this topic be in good taste?

12. After hearing a speech on this topic, what should my listeners know that they didn't before?

PLANNING THE SPEECH: AN INITIAL ASSESSMENT

<u>Evaluating Yourself As A Speaker</u>
1. What are my strengths as a speaker?
2. Do I have any potential weaknesses as a speaker?
3. How do I feel about sharing my experiences with others? That is, how much do I really want to share my ideas?
4. How do I want this audience to view me? What qualities do I want to stress?
5. Given my background and the experiences I've had, what topics could I speak on to this audience?
6. What topics would I like to investigate so that I might be better able to prepare speeches?

<u>Your Audience's View of You as a Speaker</u>
1. How does this audience appear to feel about me as a speaker?
2. Does their knowledge about me lead them to believe that I am competent? trustworthy? concerned about them as individuals?
3. Does my nonverbal communication support my oral messages with this audience? How do I know this?
4. How much does this audience know about me? Does some of their knowledge about me affect their perceptions of me as a speaker?

<u>Your Audience's View of Your Topic</u>
1. How important is this topic for my audience? Why?
2. What are the attitudes, values, and beliefs of my listeners concerning this topic?
3. Why have I selected this topic for this audience?

4. Are the people in my audience likely to listen to me? Why?

5. What special adaptations can I make to create more interest in my topic for my listeners?

6. What special purposes are the people in this audience likely to have?

7. How can I prepare this speech so that it will be important to this audience?

Your View of the Communication Situation

1. What is the physical setting likely to be for this speech?

2. What "communication rules" are likely to be operating?

3. How much time do I have to present my ideas? Will there be an opportunity for listeners to ask questions?

4. How does my speech fit into the other scheduled events? Will these affect my presentation?

5. What is the audience expecting of me?

6. How can I find out more about my audience?

Some Final Considerations

1. What is my purpose in giving this speech?

2. How extensive is my knowledge of the topic? How much research do I need to prepare myself for this presentation?

3. Am I interested in this topic? Why did I choose it?

4. Are there any special communication problems I need to consider for this speaking transaction?

A GENERAL PERFORMANCE ASSESSMENT

Name of Speaker

_____

Topic _____

THE SOURCE:

_____ poised
_____ non-apologetic
_____ accommodating
_____ firm
_____ positive self-image
_____ apparently sincere
_____ apparently concerned
_____ apparently trustworthy
_____ expert on the topic

THE MESSAGE:

_____ topic clear and significant
_____ proposition/central idea clear and significant
_____ adequate supporting material
_____ evidence adapted to audience
_____ adequate introduction
_____ adequate conclusion
_____ clear organizational pattern
_____ adequate topic development
_____ clear language
_____ vivid imagery

THE TRANSMISSION:

_____ clear articulation and enunciation
_____ volume adjusted to room
_____ vocal variation for emphasis
_____ conversational vocal delivery
_____ rate of delivery controlled
_____ non-distracting posture
_____ absence of distracting mannerisms
_____ gestures reinforced meaning/attitude
_____ non-distracting gestures
_____ reinforcing facial expression
_____ adequate eye contact
_____ unobtrusive use of notes and podium

THE RECEIVERS:

_____ their interest aroused and satisfied
_____ their previous information taken into account
_____ their attitudes recognized
_____ their presence complimented
_____ included in transaction

Comments

ASSESSMENT FORM FOR NARRATIVE SPEAKING

Name _____ Topic _____

Main Theme of Speech:

CONTENT
Clear Idea	1 2 3 4 5
Logical development	1 2 3 4 5
Adequate details	1 2 3 4 5
Summarized well	1 2 3 4 5
Within time limits	1 2 3 4 5
Other:	

PHYSICAL DELIVERY
Conversational style	1 2 3 4 5
Limited use of notes	1 2 3 4 5
Good eye contact	1 2 3 4 5
Confident poise	1 2 3 4 5
Reinforcing posture	1 2 3 4 5
Effective gestures	1 2 3 4 5
Limited distracting movement	1 2 3 4 5
Adequate enthusiasm	1 2 3 4 5
Other:	

VOCAL DELIVERY
Conversational rate	1 2 3 4 5
Effective pausing	1 2 3 4 5
Effective vocal pattern	1 2 3 4 5
Limited vocal distractions	1 2 3 4 5
Adequate volume	1 2 3 4 5
Expressiveness	1 2 3 4 5
Other:	

MAIN STRENGTH:

MAIN WEAKNESS:

TOTAL POINTS: _____

PEER RESPONSE FORM
Rate 1-5 (1=weak, 3=average,
    5=outstanding)
Speaker:
Evaluator:
CRITERIA
Delivery & Presentation
___eye contact
___voice volume
___vocal expression & inflection
___conversational tone
___gestures
___enthusiasm and/or intensity
___posture & movement
___composure
___minimal vocal distractions or physical
       habits
___visual aid handled correctly &
       effectively
Introduction
___attention
___creates reason to listen
___states purpose or central idea
Body
___ideas follow orderly fashion
___use of various form of verbal support
___transitions clear
___use of support effective
Conclusion
___adequate summary
___reached closure
Other
___audio-visual aid well chosen & well
       used
___materials adapted to audience
___topic narrowed sufficiently
___imagination & creativity

PEER RESPONSE FORM
Rate 1-5 (1=weak, 3=average,
    5=outstanding)
Speaker:
Evaluator:
CRITERIA
Delivery & Presentation
___eye contact
___voice volume
___vocal expression & inflection
___conversational tone
___gestures
___enthusiasm and/or intensity
___posture & movement
___composure
___minimal vocal distractions or physical
       habits
___visual aid handled correctly &
       effectively
Introduction
___attention
___creates reason to listen
___states purpose or central idea
Body
___ideas follow orderly fashion
___use of various form of verbal support
___transitions clear
___use of support effective
Conclusion
___adequate summary
___reached closure
Other
___audio-visual aid well chosen & well
       used
___materials adapted to audience
___topic narrowed sufficiently

PEER RESPONSE FORM
Rate 1-5 (1=weak, 3=average,
5=outstanding)
Speaker:
Evaluator:
CRITERIA
<u>Delivery & Presentation</u>
___eye contact
___voice volume
___vocal expression & inflection
___conversational tone
___gestures
___enthusiasm and/or intensity
___posture & movement
___composure
___minimal vocal distractions or physical habits
___visual aid handled correctly & effectively
<u>Introduction</u>
___attention
___creates reason to listen
___states purpose or central idea
<u>Body</u>
___ideas follow orderly fashion
___use of various form of verbal support
___transitions clear
___use of support effective
<u>Conclusion</u>
___adequate summary
___reached closure
<u>Other</u>
___audio-visual aid well chosen & well used
___materials adapted to audience
___topic narrowed sufficiently
___imagination & creativity

EVALUATION FORM
Name:
Topic:
Occasion: **Speech length**

Introduction (15 points)
Gained audience's attention
Established Speaker's credibility and good will
Revealed nature of topic as central idea or claim
Prepared audience for rest of speech (forecasting)

Body (40 points)
Main points clearly identified
Each main point developed with appropriate materials
Topic development appropriate for this occasion, audience
Logical arrangement of ideas
Transitions used effectively
Appropriate support (examples, testimony, statistics) used
Clear source citation
Relation to and inclusion of audience
Appropriate use of visual aids (if needed/used)

Conclusion (15 points)
Prepared audience for end
Reinforced central idea or claim in an appropriate manner

Presentation and Delivery (30 points)
Extemporaneous delivery
Enthusiasm for subject
Gestures/movements appropriate
Facial expressions appropriate
Eye contact appropriate
Pronunciation clear, accurate
Appropriate word choice for occasion, audience
Vocal variety
Fluent expression

[Adapted from Carlson and Smith-Howell]

CHAPTER 3.   SETTING THE SCENE FOR COMMUNITY IN A DIVERSE CULTURE: PUBLIC SPEAKING AND CRITICAL LISTENING

CHAPTER CONTENT

> Basic Elements of the Speechmaking Process: A Model Overview
> > The Speaker
> > The Message
> > The Listener
> > Feedback
> > The Channels
> > The Situation
> > *Communication Research Dateline: Listening and Your Career: Working across the Generational Gap*
> > The Cultural Context
> Critical Listening: Theory and Practice
> > Knowing Purposes: An Orientation to Listening Behaviors
> > Critical Listening for Comprehension and Judgment
> The Ethical Listener
> > *How to Be an Active and Ethical Listener*
> Taking Good Notes
> Special Needs for Critical Listening in the Classroom
> Chapter Summary
> Key Terms
> Assessment Activities
> References

Discussion Questions

1.   Draw a model of the communication transaction. Explain your drawing.
2.   What is self-image? How does it affect the speech situation?
3.   What is speaker credibility? ethos?
4.   What does research tell us about the role of credibility in public speaking?
5.   What three variables make up the speaker's message?
6.   What are some of the reasons listeners enter speech transactions?
7.   What is audience analysis?
8.   What is feedback?

9. What are the channels of communication? Explain each.
10. What are the elements that make up the situation?
11. How does the social context of a speech affect the speaker?
12. What are communication rules?
13. When do cultural rules and expectations become important?
14. What is communication competence?
15. What do we mean when we call public speaking a "communication transaction?"
16. How important is listening as part of communication activity?
17. What two kinds of feedback do listeners provide?
18. Give an example of immediate feedback and delayed feedback.
19. What is listening?
20. Distinguish the RRP, VAT, and SUR styles of listening.
21. Why are inferences about someone's apparent poor listening sometimes inaccurate?
22. What are some of the key differences in situations that require appreciative rather than discriminative listening or therapeutic listening rather than just listening for comprehension?
23. Which kinds of listening are you most likely to use in your daily life?
24. What is the difference between active and reflective listening?
25. What does it mean to be an ethical listener?
26. What questions will help you to comprehend messages when you listening for comprehension?
27. Explain the R.R.A. Technique. What is the purpose of the RRA Technique?
28. What questions should you ask when assessing the speech situation?
29. What questions should you ask when assessing the speaker?
30. What questions should you ask when assessing the message?
31. Explain how you can become a better note taker.
32. What advice would you give someone who wanted to develop a good note-taking scheme?
33. How can you improve your listening skills during this course?

Questions to Stimulate Critical Thinking

1. How can the communication model presented aid in your understanding of the communication process?
2. How can you tell whether your image of the "other" and that person's image of "self" are similar, or even on the same planet?
3. How might you assess audience feedback -- what cues are they likely to give you and how can you be sure you interpret their cues accurately?
4. Using either the RRP, VAT or SUR approaches to listening styles, how might a speaker facilitate audience listening?
5. What attributes of messages might enhance their effectiveness for listeners?

6.   Whose responsibility is effective listening--the speaker's or the audience's?

7.   Speculate about how much of our listening potential do we typically utilize? Defend your answer.

8.   What can a speaker say to increase the motivation of audience members to listen?

9.   What environmental elements can affect your desire to listen to a message? Whose responsibility is it to control those environmental elements? In particular consider the environmental constraints on listening present in your classroom.

10.   What implications does the kind of listening you are engaged in as a member of an audience have for you?

11.   What are some solutions to listeners' tendencies to "drop out?"

12.   Provide several examples of how the public speaker might engage his or her listeners in therapeutic listening.

13.   What can a public speaker do to aid in overcoming the poor listening habits of his/her listeners?

14.   How is appreciative listening different from discriminative listening, therapeutic listening, critical listening?

15.   Think of several recent examples of public messages that were hindered or enhanced by strong or weak listening skills.

16.   Can trigger words we used by speakers to circumvent their audience members' critical listening skills? Identify several examples. Is this ethical?

17.   Some research suggests that the complexity of an individual's cognitive processes is responsible for differences in listening comprehension. Explain what you think the relationship might be.

Application Exercises

1. The Communication Process:
   A. Objective: To identify elements of the process of communication in realistic settings.
   B. Procedure: Following a short discussion of the elements in the process of communication, ask students to identify those elements in situations such as the following:
      1) A telephone conversation
      2) A person reading a newspaper silently
      3) A president addressing a national audience via television
      4) Three roommates discussing a date
      5) A student speaker in your classroom
      6) An E-mail message sent to a friend
   C. Discussion: What are the similarities and differences among the various communication situations? Are some elements of communication present in all or most forms of communication?

2. Original Models of Communication

    A. Objective: To enhance understanding of the functions and forms of communication models.

    B. Procedure: Divide students into small groups of three or four. Ask each group to develop a model of communication that reflects what the group considers to be the important relationships among the elements in the communication process. Divide the chalkboard into sections and ask a representative from each group to draw the group model on the board. Taking turns, a member from each group should explain the model to the rest of the class.

    C. Discussion: How do the models differ? Are certain elements in the communication process constant? How does each model present a unique view of communication? How can models help us understand communication?

3. Distinguishing the Listening Styles

    A. Objective: To clarify the differences among the three Listening Styles discussed. B. Procedure: After students have read the chapter, divide the chalkboard into three sections. Write RRP, VAT, and SUR at the top of each section. Ask students what strategy or strategies they might use in addressing each listening style.

    C. Discussion: What are the differences? Similarities?

4. Listening for Comprehension and Judgment

    A. Objective: To stimulate students' awareness of the various ways in which they may listen for comprehension and judgment.

    B. Procedure: Spend a few minutes reviewing the distinctions between the purposes for listening. Then divide the class into groups of 4-6 students and assign each group the task of listing as many examples as possible of either one kind of listening/of all forms of listening. To provide a game flavor for this exercise and get them involved, you might give the groups a time limit and/or reward the group with the longest list of examples. At the end of the assigned time, ask a spokesperson from each group to read the group's list. You might also save the lists and use examples from them as quiz or examination items.

    C. Discussion: Are the examples classified accurately according to their purpose? What is the purpose of each form of listening? To what extent are each of the forms of listening used in a typical day? Which forms of listening are used most often? Why?

5. Practice Listening Drill

    A. Objective: To increase students' awareness of listening as a skill.

    B. Procedure: Play a 5-6 minute segment of a video or audiotaped newscast. At the conclusion of the tape, ask students to write down what they recall from the tape. Ask selected members of the class to read their answers.

C. Discussion: What did everyone recall about the newscast? Why? What were the differences in individuals' listening patterns? Did you have more or less difficulty with the exercise than others in the class? Why? After re-playing the tape, ask the following questions--what did you miss the first time you "heard" the newscast? Why? Were you an impartial listener? Did you employ a different listening behavior the second time you "heard" the tape?

6. Getting There

A. Objective: To demonstrate the value of listener feedback.

B. Procedure: Provide a volunteer with a map. Ask the volunteer to locate a point on the map and give directions to the rest of the class. Ask the class to draw their own maps as the directions are given. You may try these variations:

> 1) Minimal Feedback: Require the speaker to face away from the audience and forbid listeners to make any noise or in any other way influence the speaker.
>
> 2) Maximum Feedback: Allow the speaker to face the listeners and allow listeners to ask questions or otherwise interact with the speaker.
>
> 3) Minimal Detail: Give the speaker a time limit for providing directions. One to three minutes should be effective.
>
> 4) Maximum Detail: Encourage the speaker to provide elaborate details. Do not impose a time limit.

C. Discussion: Compare the maps. What differences do you detect? How could the directions have been clearer? What is the value of feedback in the speaking situation? What types of feedback can listeners provide? How important is detail in improving audience understanding? What differences in perception did you detect among listeners?

7. Note Taking Assessment

A. Objective: To evaluate note taking skills.

B. Procedure: Ask each student to take out their notebooks for the most recent lecture in this class. Divide them into small groups and have them compare notes with other students.

C. Discussion: What gaps did you discover in your notes? Were you trying to write down everything that was said? Were you able to identify and write down the main points? What format did you use to record your notes? Did you use abbreviations effectively? Did you leave enough space so that you can add facts and marginal notes later? Did you use color coding in your notes? Do your notes indicate that you are a passive or active listener? How often should you review your notes in preparation for examinations? You might follow up this exercise by comparing note taking after studying listening behavior. Can you see a difference?

8. Additional Exercise: Ask students to fill out the Listener Self-Assessment Sheet at the end of this chapter. Discuss their responses.

Impromptu Speaking Activities

1. Chain Impromptu
    A. Objective: To integrate the textbook theory directly into a speaking activity.
    B. Procedure: Start the chain by making several impromptu remarks to the group. Your comments can have a theme such as favorite meals, home town or recreational activities. As soon as you have concluded your impromptu speech, choose another person in the classroom to speak.   That person should refer to something you said in his/her impromptu remarks. The result should be that each student listens closely to what the speaker is saying.

2. Listening Quiz
    A. Objective: To increase students' awareness that listening is a continuous process in which they engage.
    B. Procedure: At the conclusion of a class discussion or lecture in which students have listened closely to detailed material, pass out prepared questions. Ask each student to answer one or more of the questions in a brief impromptu speech. To discover how listening may vary, you may ask several students to answer the same question.

Additional Resources

Armstrong, Lindsley and Peter Kellett. "Teaching Public Speaking Principles Through Impromptu Speaking." The Speech Communication Teacher 9 (1995): 5.

Barker, Larry Lee and Kittie Watson. Listen Up : How to Improve Relationships, Reduce Stress, and Be More Productive by Using the Power of Listening. Bedford, MA: St. Martin's Press, 2000.

Burns, Mari Miller, "Listening for Hallmark." Communication Teacher15 (2001):11-12.

Cichon, Elaine J., "Practicing Active Listening." Communication Teacher16 (2000):11-14.

Crandall, Heather, "Practicing Impromptu Speeches," Speech Communication Teacher 13 (1999): 3-4.

Kimble, James. "The Big Mouth Speakoff." Speech Communication Teacher 9 (1995): 1-2.

Mallard, Kina S. "The Listening Box," Speech Communication Teacher 12 (1997): 9.

Shultz, Kara. "MTV Impromptu." Speech Communication Teacher 10 (1995): 5-6.

Taylor, Jackie, "Learning Styles: A practical Tool for Improved Communications." Supervision 59 (1998):18-19.

Wolvin, Andrew and Carolyn Coakley. "A Survey of the Status of Listening Training in Some Fortune 500 Corporations." Communication Education 40 (1991): 152-164.

Wolvin, Andrew D. and Carolyn Gwynn Coakley, (Eds.), Perspectives on Listening. Norwood, NJ: Ablex Publishing Company, 1993.

Wolvin, Andrew D. and Carolyn Gwynn Coakley, (Eds.), Listening. 5th Ed., NY: McGraw-Hill, 1995.

LISTENER SELF-ASSESSMENT FORM

1.   Am I a good listener? Why do I feel this way?

2.   Do I find it hard to listen to topics that I'm not interested in?

3.   What topics bore me?

4.   What habits of speakers annoy me?

5.   Do I react to specific words and ideas? What are they?

6.   Do I find myself daydreaming while people are speaking to me?

7.   Do I tend to "debate" ideas in my own mind while a speaker is talking? What impact does this have on my ability to listen?

8.   Do I want people to listen to me when I am speaking? What strategies do I employ to create attention in my listeners?

ABILITY TO FOLLOW DIRECTIONS

TIME: 10 Minutes
           Name _____

The object of this exam will point out that directions are made to be followed. Trainees often find difficulty with an assignment not because they can't do the work, but because they have not followed directions. They have not followed directions because they have not read them carefully enough to fully understand. This would not be wise, because the main direction is this: READ EVERYTHING BEFORE DOING ANYTHING.

1. Print your last name in the space provided on this page where it says "Name."
2. Circle the word "provided" in sentence one.
3. Draw five small squares in the upper left-hand corner of this page.
4. Put an "X" in each square.
5. Put a circle around each square.
6. Underline "ability to follow directions."
7. After "ability to follow directions," write "Yes."
8. Put a circle around "each" in sentence five.
9. Put an "X" in the lower left-hand corner of this page.
10. Draw a triangle around the "X" that you have just drawn.
11. Draw a rectangle around the word "square" in sentence three.
12. On the reverse side of this paper, in the upper left-hand corner, add 50 and 40.
13. On the reverse side of this paper, at the top right-hand corner, multiply 70 by 98.
14. Write your first name before doing anything else on this test.
15. If you think you have followed directions up to this point, write "I have."
16. Now that you have followed the directions in the first paragraph to READ EVERYTHING BEFORE DOING ANYTHING, do only sentence one

[Copied from State of Wisconsin Dept. Of Workforce Development Web site: http://www.dwd.state.wi.us/notespub/dwdpub/2246_28a.htm
Publication Number: DWE-9482]

Note: The following page can be copied for distribution in class; present the instructions **orally** to the class as you begin to hand out the form: "In filling this out, read everything before doing anything."

ABILITY TO FOLLOW DIRECTIONS

TIME: 10 Minutes

Name _____

1. Print your last name in the space provided on this page where it says "Name."

2. Circle the word "provided" in sentence one.

3. Draw five small squares in the upper left-hand corner of this page.

4. Put an "X" in each square.

5. Put a circle around each square.

6. Underline "ability to follow directions."

7. After "ability to follow directions," write "Yes."

8. Put a circle around "each" in sentence five.

9. Put an "X" in the lower left-hand corner of this page.

10. Draw a triangle around the "X" that you have just drawn.

11. Draw a rectangle around the word "square" in sentence three.

12. On the reverse side of this paper, in the upper left-hand corner, add 50 and 40.

13. On the reverse side of this paper, at the top right-hand corner, multiply 70 by 98.

14. Write your first name before doing anything else on this test.

15. If you think you have followed directions up to this point, write "I have."

16. Now that you have followed the directions in the first paragraph to READ EVERYTHING BEFORE DOING ANYTHING, do only sentence one

CHAPTER 4.   PUBLIC SPEAKING AND CULTURAL LIFE

CHAPTER CONTENT

Understanding Cultural Processes
  Orality and Cultural Life
  The Dimensions of Culture
  The Challenge of Speaking in a Multicultural Society
Strategies for Unifying Multicultural Audiences
  Recognizing Diversity
  Negotiating Multicultural Values
  Accepting Multiple Paths to Goals
  Communication Research Dateline: Rhetorical Framing
  Working Through the Lifestyle Choices of Others
  Maintaining Self-Identity in the Face of Difference
  Ethical Moments: Adapting to Moral Codes
Chapter Summary
Key Terms
Assessment Activities
References

Discussion Questions

1.   What is the meaning of "culture?"
2.   How is orality connected to culture?
3.   What does it mean to say speech is "integrative" and "traditionalist?"
4.   Of the 7 features of oral speech, which is the most critical in your experience?
5.   What is distinctive about culture as "lived?"
6.   What is the meant by multiculturalism?
7.   What is distinctive about culture as "thought?"
8.   What is meant by ideology? Hegemony?
9.   What is distinctive about culture as "performed?"
10. What is the difference between embodiment and enactment?
11. What is distinctive about recognizing culture as a communication strategy?
12. What is distinctive about negotiating culture as a communication strategy?
13. How can one use information about value orientations in negotiating culture?
14. What is distinctive about accepting multiple paths within culture as a communication strategy?

15.   What is distinctive about working through culture as a communication strategy?
16.   What is distinctive about maintaining self-identity as a communication strategy?.

Questions to Stimulate Critical Thinking

1.   What are some of the important co-cultures that students might interact with on a college campus?
2.   How might communication change as one moves in and out of co-cultures?
3.   Some scholars have suggested that persons of color often 'code-switch' as they move between their co-culture and the 'mainstream' culture (as in African-Americans moving between their home and their professional work). What accounts for the code-switching?
4.   What impact has 'culture as lived' had on your life?
5.   What are some examples of how ideology and hegemony work to influence culture?
6.   What are some ways in which different cultures express their values?
7.   What are some of the ways in which one can communicate recognition of diverse cultures?
8.   What are some of the ways in which we might negotiate difference while achieving unity?
9.   Does achieving unity mean the erasure of difference? How might that be avoided if it were to mean erasure?
10.   Why is it important to adopt the lifestyles of others in some settings -- what would be some situations in which a communicator might find that useful? When might it backfire?
11.   Why is it important to maintain self-identity when negotiating difference? What would be some situations in which a communicator might be challenged in maintaining identity?

Application Exercises

1. Diversity Awareness
      A. Objective: To increase awareness of cultural diversity in a student's social setting.
      B. Procedure: Depending on the cultural diversity of your own class, have students research the ethnic makeup of the campus -- what other cultures are represented, and in what proportion of the general population? Also, have students research the proportion of co-cultures within the State.
      C. Discussion: How well does the campus reflect the State's diversity (the nation's?). What kinds of experiences have students had in communicating interpersonally with others?

2. Culture as Lived/Thought
      A. Objective: To enhance understanding of culture as 'lived', 'thought' and 'performed.'
      B. Procedure: Working in small groups, have students discuss the kinds of rules that regulate their own lives (judicial - speeding, stopping at stop signs; social - coming to

class without showering first; political - voting). Ask each group to list the various rules that govern their living from day to day.

    C. Discussion: What are the 'taken for granted' rules that govern the everyday lives of students? How might these affect different cultures as they are experienced (as in the case of 'racial profiling' --how does this practice affect different cultures?)?

3. Creating Unity from Diversity

    A. Objective: To increase awareness of the strategies that may be used to appreciate difference while achieving unity.

    B. Procedure: Have students select a controversy related to community or campus life; depending on the diversity of the class, have them go out and interview representatives from other cultures (from co-cultures within the U. S. to international cultures). The goal is to see how these interviewees see the issue.

    C. Discussion: What differences, if any, are there between the views of students in class and those interviewed? To what extent are the views dependent on different cultural values? What kinds of strategies might work best in recognizing and working through alternate views?

4. Knowing other cultures

    A. Objective: To gain experience with other cultural perspectives.

    B. Procedure: Have students select a culture they are previously unfamiliar with. Have them do some research on communication customs in that country -- what are some of the 'do's and 'don'ts' of communicating in that culture? Have the students report their findings in class (this also can be a small group activity). [See Morrison, et al. in Resource list below]

    C. Discussion: When is it critical, based on the review, to 'adopt the lifestyle' of the other culture in communicating? Why is it important to be aware of cultural differences related to communication?

Impromptu Speaking Activities

1. Rules for Living

    A. Objective: To recognize the role of hegemony in everyday cultural experience.

    B. Procedure: Using judicial, social and political arenas as the main categories, ask each student to think of and speak for 2 minutes on a 'rule for living' from the judicial, social or political arena that affects their personal lives -- vary the categories as you move from student to student. This will get easier for students as you move through the exercise.

2. Code Switching

    A. Objective: To increase students' awareness of talking differently across contexts.

    B. Procedure: Ask students to give an example of their own experience in talking differently in different contexts. This can be a small group activity, to decrease the amount of time some students have to think about their own 'story.' It has the added advantage of getting students to know each other relatively early in the term if they are working in small groups, with each taking turns presenting a 'story.' Relate their experiences as an analog to different cultural experiences -- how well do they think the analogy holds?

Additional Resources

Bradford, Lisa and Deborah Uecker, "Intercultural Simulations." Speech Communication Teacher 13 (1999): 1-7.

Brunson, Deborah A., "Talking about Race by Talking about Whiteness." Communication Teacher 14 (2000):1-4.

Galvin, K. M. and P. Cooper, (Eds.), Making Connections. Los Angeles, CA: Roxbury, 1996.

Hecht, M, M. Collier, and S. Ribeau, (Eds.), African-American Communication: Ethnic Identity and Cultural Interpretation. Newbury Park, CA: Sage, 1993.

Martin, Judith N. and Tom K. Nakayama, Intercultural Communication in Contexts. Mountain View, CA: Mayfield, 1997.

Miller, Ann Neville, "Cultural Partners: Diversity and Intercultural Communication Beyond the Classroom." Speech Communication Teacher 13 (1999): 12-13.

Morrison, Terri, Wayne A. Conaway and George A. Borden, Kiss, Bow, or Shake Hands: How to Do Business in Sixty Countries. Holbrook, MA: Adams Media Corp., 1994.

Schrader, Stuart M. "Increasing Cultural Awareness: Importance of Story Telling in Speech Making." Speech Communication Teacher 13(1999): 8-9.

Yook, Eunkyong Lee and Rosita D. Albert, "Perceptions of International Teaching Assistants: The Interrelatedness of Intercultural Training, Cognition, and Emotion." Communication Education 48 (1999):1-17

NEGOTIATING CULTURAL DIFFERENCES

The following examples provide illustrations of how communication might go awry in different cultures. Using these illustrations, engage students in a discussion of other differences that they have noted in their own experiences, or combine this with the 'research' task in Application Exercise # 4.

1. During the 1988 Summer Olympics, a T-Shirt with "We're Bad" and a drawing showing boxers with the South Korean flag as background was deemed offensive by South Koreans. The slogan, made popular by Michael Jackson, was taken literally, and the use of the flag was seen as demeaning a country.

2. The otherwise innocent use of "thank God," expressed in an Islamic or Buddhist culture, may be taken as blasphemy unless meant in a clearly religious sense; in the Middle East, saying Inshallah (God willing) is perceived positively as it suggests some familiarity with their religion and customs.

3. After suggesting "tabling" an item, the American was surprised when his London counterpart immediately began discussing the issue. The term has an opposite meaning in English culture.

4. Saying "you" in a high-level discussion with Japanese businessmen is a violation of their expectation not to be addressed directly.

5. Pointing an index finger in stressing an idea is considered impolite in Middle and Far Eastern cultures.

6. Expressing praise with a "thumbs up" gesture is considered rude in Australia.

7. Eat only with the right hand if you are in an Arab country or in the home of any Muslim; receive and pass food only with the right hand in India; never use the left hand to touch food. The left hand is considered unclean.

8. While we have coined "the Persian Gulf" with reference to the recent war in that area, don't use that expression in the Gulf States--the body of water referred to is termed the Arabian Gulf by them.

9. Addressing a Japanese businessman by his first name suggests a familiarity that is reserved for family and close friends.

10. In Pakistan, it is considered impolite to discuss business during dinner.

[Adapted from Roger E. Axtell, Do's and Taboos Around the World. 2nd Ed., New York: Wiley, 1990; originally printed in James Benjamin and Raymie E. McKerrow, Business and Professional Communication: Concepts and Practices. New York: HarperCollins, 1994, p. 87]

CHAPTER 5.   ANALYZING THE AUDIENCE AND OCCASION

CHAPTER CONTENT

Analyzing Audiences Demographically
    Analyzing Demographic Categories
    Using Demographic Information
Analyzing Audiences Psychologically
    Beliefs
    Attitudes
    Values
    Desires, Visions, and Fantasies
    Using a Psychological Profile
Analyzing the Speech Occasion
Using Audience Analysis in Speech Preparation
    How to Analyze the Speech Occasion
    Audience Targeting: Setting Realistic Goals
    Audience Segmentation: Selecting Dominant Ideas and Appeals
    Creating A Unifying Vision or Fantasy
    Ethical Moments: Analyzing Audience and Occasion in Moments of Controversy
    Sample Audience Analysis
Chapter Summary
Key Terms
Assessment Activities
References

Discussion Questions

1. What does it mean when we say public speaking is "audience and occasion centered?"
2. What is the goal of audience analysis?
3. What is demographic analysis?
4. Identify and describe each of the demographic characteristics of an audience.
5. What is key in using demographic information discovered about an audience?
6. Why should a speaker understand the psychological profile of an audience?
7. What are the differences between demographic and psychological characteristics of audiences?
8. What are beliefs?
9. Distinguish fact from opinion; fixed from variable beliefs.
10. What is a stereotype? Give several examples.
11. Why is it important to understand the kind of beliefs audience members may hold?
12. What are attitudes? Provide several examples.
13. What are values? terminal values? instrumental values?
14. What are value orientations or ideologies? How do they affect a speaker's subject or purpose?
15. What is a rhetorical vision? How does public speaking contribute to rhetorical visions?

16.   How can you use the information you gather about your audience's beliefs, attitudes, values, and rhetorical visions as you develop your speech?
17.   What are the characteristics of the speech occasion?
18.   What occasion factors must a speaker take into consideration when planning a speech? How does each factor affect the choices made by the speaker?
19.   What two forms do audience expectations take?
20.   What choices does a speaker have when facing strong audience expectations?
21.   What should the speaker consider when analyzing the speech occasion?
22.   What considerations are relevant when targeting your audience?
23.   What is audience segmentation? How can an understanding of audience segmentation aid the speaker in selecting materials for the speech?
24.   What is a valuative vocabulary? Give several examples.
25.   How can a speaker create a rhetorical vision?

Questions to Stimulate Critical Thinking

1.   How accurately do you think a speaker can determine an audience's psychological profile?
2.   How do you think audience membership affects an individual's beliefs, attitudes, and values?
3.   What is the relationship between beliefs, attitudes, and values and human behavior?
.   How much do you think basic values are subject to change during an individual's lifetime?
5.   Some people argue that basic values are dramatically challenged during an individual's adolescence. Do you agree? Why or why not?
6.   If you were a member of an audience, what important characteristics do you think a speaker should know about your demographic and psychological make-up? How similar are you and your classmates in this respect?
7.   To what extent is it the speaker's obligation to appeal to an audience's higher values?
8.   What makes the speech occasion different from most other occasions?
9.   Think of a speech occasion in which the speaker violated the audience expectations. Was the speaker successful? Why or why not?
10.   Can you identify any situations when the speaker should ignore audience expectations and the demands of the speaking situation?
11.   To what extent does the judgment of speaking competence depend on the audience expectations rather than on the skill or preparation of the speaker?
12.   List several rhetorical visions present in our society. What contributes to the maintenance of these visions?

Application Exercises

1. Psyching Out Your Audience
    A. Objective: To better understand both your classmates as audience members and the concepts of beliefs, attitudes, and values.
    B. Procedure: After a brief discussion of the terms beliefs, attitudes, and values, choose one or more topics which students might consider for your classroom. Divide the chalkboard into three columns labeling each with one of the terms. With students'

cooperation attempt to identify and record their beliefs, attitudes, and values in the appropriate columns.

C. Discussion: To what extent is the audience homogeneous or heterogeneous in each of the psychological factors? Do relationships exist between beliefs, attitudes, and values? Is there a correspondence between psychological and demographic factors? What variables might alter the beliefs? attitudes? values?

2. Adapting to the Audience

A. Objective: To increase students' awareness of audience variation.

B. Procedure: Ask students to identify 2-3 different audiences or provide examples for them. You might suggest, for example, a national television audience, a Veterans of Foreign Wars group, or participants in the Special Olympics. For each of these audiences, assign three groups to identify demographic factors, psychological factors, and audience segments and then, report the conclusions of each group.

C. Discussion: Compare the observations of each group. Discuss the impact this audience analysis would have on a speaker's choice of topic/purpose.

3. Valuative Vocabulary

A. Objective: To extend the student's understanding of audience analysis as an important factor in phrasing the speech.

B. Procedure: Using a mock audience such as one in the preceding exercise, identify the demographic and psychological factors for the audience as a whole and for each segment of it. Then, develop valuative vocabulary intended to motivate attention for each of the groups identified.

C. Discussion: Stress the interrelationship among the variables of audience analysis and speaker's choices of vocabulary. It is useful to tie in the concepts of language abstraction, intensity, and gender-neutral word choices at this point.

4. Adapting the Central Idea/Claim to the Audience

A. Objective: To stress the interrelationships of speaker purpose and audience through central idea/claim.

B. Procedure: Provide a general speech subject for which students have some basic knowledge such as a current campus issue. Describe several potential audiences for a speaker and ask groups of 4-5 students to provide a central idea/claim statement for the speaker.

C. Discussion: Analyze how effective each central idea/claim is likely to be considering the targeted audience. Also note the factors which influenced the development of the statement.

5. Developing a Psychological Profile of the Class

A. Objective: To determine the beliefs, attitudes, and values of the class.

B. Procedure: Ask students to list three to five things that they think their classmates believe. Give each student a chance to read their list. Ask if the class agrees or determine by a show of hands how many students agree with each item on the list.

C. Discussion: What assumptions were made about the class? What are those assumptions based on? What group tendencies should be noted? How did students reach their conclusions about the beliefs, attitudes, and values of the class?

6. Who Reads <u>Newsweek</u>?
    A. Objective: To develop an understanding of audience segmentation.
    B. Procedure: Choose a current issue of a popular news magazine such as <u>Newsweek</u>, <u>Time</u>, or <u>U.S. News</u>. Select several advertisements from that issue to analyze. Develop a demographic and psychological profile of the audience from the advertisements.
    C. Discussion: What verbal and visual appeals are being used to persuade readers to purchase products? What consistent appeals did you find in the advertisements? What kind of reader do these appeals suggest? How would these advertisements differ if they were intended to persuade a different audience?

7. Additional Applications: Ask students to assess their classroom audience using the audience analysis form included in this chapter. Complete the Audience Analysis Exercise included in this chapter.

Impromptu Speaking Activities

1. "This is a Public Service Announcement"
    A. Objective: To encourage students to think of the audience as an important influence on the speaker's choices of topic and purpose.
    B. Procedure: Provide the class with a description of a fictitious audience and ask each student to think of a public service announcement aimed at that audience. In a short impromptu explanation, each student will reveal the announcement and the reasons it is adapted well to the fictitious audience.

2. Varying the Audience
    A. Objective: To stimulate students' understanding of the process of adapting appeals to meet the needs of an audience.
    B. Procedure: Have each student write down the general characteristics of an audience/occasion - have them include the purpose for the gathering, the size and composition of the audience (e.g., Sr. Citizen's Ctr. Meeting to hear from college students on their plans for volunteering their services; 20 men over 70, 10 women over 70, mixed ethnic backgrounds). They then hand their audience profile to the person next to them. The speaker is to adapt a 2-3 minute impromptu presentation to the profile the student has created [to avoid some students having more time than others to prepare, stagger the "handoff" of profiles].

3. Predicting the Future
    A. Objective: To vary the classroom speaker's audience and the speech occasion.
    B. Procedure: Ask your students to imagine that they are ten years into the future and are describing the career they have chosen to a group of high school dropouts, elementary school children, senior citizens, peers, etc. (the student should choose an audience or you may assign varied audiences). Each student should briefly describe their job to the audience.

Additional Resources

Ajzen, Icek and Martin Fishbein. <u>Understanding Attitudes and Predicting Social Behaviors</u>.
    Englewood Cliffs, NJ: Prentice Hall, 1997.
McClarty, W. "Audience Analysis: Go and Tell." <u>Speech Communication Teacher</u> 8 (1993):
    4-5.
Mohsen, Raed. "Out on Campus: A Challenging Public Speaking Experience." <u>Speech
    Communication Teacher</u> 7 (1993): 10-11.
Neumann, David. "Selecting Messages: An Exercise in Audience Analysis." <u>Speech
    Communication Teacher</u> 4 (1990): 9.
Stern, Rick. "Audience Spinouts." <u>Speech Communication Teacher</u> 5 (1991): 7-8.

AUDIENCE ASSESSMENT SHEET

Name _____

What is the nature of the speaking occasion?

What is the composition of this audience?
    Size:
    Age:
    Gender:
    Occupation:
    Education:
    Group memberships:
    Cultural-Ethnic background:
What is their knowledge of the subject area?

What are their general beliefs, attitudes, and values?
    Political:
    Professional:
    Economic:
    Social:
    Religious:
    Other pertinent areas:

What is their general attitude toward me as a speaker?

What is their general attitude toward the speech purpose?

Given this analysis, how should I prepare my presentation?

AUDIENCE ANALYSIS EXERCISE

Consider each of the following situations. Think of a speech topic and general speech purpose. Then determine how you would adapt each speech topic and purpose to the situation.

Situation #1

Evening meeting of local Rotary Club; 30 male and 20 female members range in age from 22-59; all religious denominations are represented; members are predominantly white and middle to upper income levels; most are business persons; one is a high school principal; all have some college education. Meeting time: 1 hour Speaking time: 15 minutes Place: St. Mary's Church basement

Situation #2

Young Republicans local chapter meeting; 97 members are 18-23 years old; mostly Protestant from suburban communities; all are college students; half are women, half are men, mostly white with a few African Americans. Meeting time: 2 hours Speaking time: 20 minutes Place: University Center

Situation #3

Monthly meeting of Local 109--a local union of workers in a variety of business settings but mainly in collections, accounting, and bookkeeping. Members are all women ranging in age from 19-62; mixed ethnic backgrounds; average annual wage $26,000; education level from eighth grade through high school; attendance required. Meeting time: 1 hour Speaking time: 15 minutes Place: local community center meeting room

Situation #4

Annual meeting of Ministers' Neighborhood Action Alliance--a group of ministers who have formed to fight drug abuse in urban neighborhoods. Members are predominantly black ministers from fundamentalist and evangelical religious groups; ages range from 27-45; most have some theological training. Meeting time: 3 day conference Speaking time: 30 minutes Place: local church

Situation #5

Local volunteer organization formed to manage donated clothes collected and disbursed from the Senior Citizen's Center. Most members are working women of varied backgrounds. Some have college educations and belong to other service groups or volunteer time elsewhere. Meeting time: 1 hour Speaking time: 20 minutes Place: Sr. Citizen's Center

ADAPTING TO AUDIENCES

Determine how you would approach each audience situation below. Be sure to analyze each audience for both demographic characteristics (size, gender, age, educational level, group membership, cultural & ethnic background) and internal psychological characteristics (beliefs, attitudes & values).

1. You have been asked to address a group of faculty members on the issue of increasing minority recruitment within the college, especially in business and communication. What appeals would you make that may assist in gaining a greater diversity of students within these (or other) disciplines?

2. It's Fire Prevention Week in your hometown and the local Fire Department has volunteered to address grades 1-6 in a local elementary school on safety. What advice would you give the Fire Department spokesperson?

3. You are a salesperson in a John Deere dealership and have several farmers gathered to see the latest equipment. Unfortunately, farm product prices have fallen drastically lately and several local farm foreclosures have occurred. What strategies might work to enlist this audience's interest?

5. There has been a recent outbreak of racial discord in your community. As a local council member, you have been invited to address a meeting of local concerned citizens on how the city will respond and insure the safety of citizens. How will you handle the diverse interests that will be present at this meeting?

6. You are talking with a group of potential pledges to your sorority/fraternity. Their excellent scholastic records, musical talent, and personalities make them the targets of numerous competing sororities/fraternities. What would you say to get them to join your organization?

7. There have been recent attacks on gay members of your university community. You are speaking at a rally to urge the university to do more to protect all students, irrespective of sexual orientation. What appeals do you use?

CHAPTER 6. DEVELOPING IDEAS: FINDING AND USING SUPPORTING MATERIALS

CHAPTER CONTENT

Discussion Questions

1. What is the key to successfully searching for supporting materials?
2. What is the purpose of supporting material?
3. Identify and describe each of the six kinds of supporting materials available to the speaker.
4. Provide an example of each kind of supporting material.
5. What considerations should be kept in mind when selecting illustrations and narratives?
6. How is a specific instance different from an illustration?
7. Distinguish among magnitudes, segments, and trends? When would you use each?
8. What guidelines should a speaker keep in mind when using statistics as supporting material?
9. What criteria should testimony satisfy when it is used as supporting material?
10. What are common electronic sources of supporting materials?

11.   What are common print sources of supporting materials?
12.   What is the primary goal of an informational interview?
13.   What guidelines should interviewers observe when planning informational interviews?
14.   What advice would you give a friend who wants to record information in a useable form?
15.   What is plagiarism?
16.   How can you avoid plagiarism?

Questions to Stimulate Critical Thinking

1.   How does the oral citation of supporting material interact with speaker credibility?
2.   Are all numbers statistics? Why or why not?
3.   We frequently hear the claim that it's easy to lie with statistics. Explain how statistics can misrepresent the truth.
4.   Think of something that you consider to be true. What kind of supporting material would it take to influence you to change your mind? Compare your answers with those of others. Are they similar? different? Why?
5.   Do you think the effectiveness of supporting material depends, in part, on the audience? Why or why not?
6.   What are the strengths and weaknesses of each kind of supporting material? How can a speaker maximize the strengths and minimize the weaknesses of each?
7.   Identify what you consider to be the weakest and strongest forms of supporting material. Justify your answer. Consider whether the strength of supporting materials lies with the perception of receivers.
8.   If you are planning a speech to your peers on the problems of alcoholism between university and college students, what kinds of supporting materials should you use? Justify your choices. Do your choices change if you discover that several of your listeners are alcoholics? Why or why not?
9.   Recently, noted historians Stephen Ambrose and Doris Kearns Goodwin have been accused of plagiarizing portions of their new books from older works by other authors. What harm is there if these allegations are true (and they appear to be)?
10.   What communicative skills are essential for a successful interview?
11.   Do you think all cultures view the forms of supporting material the same way? Why or why not?
12.   When adapting material from the Internet, what should you look for in being certain the information is reliable and accurate?

Application Exercises

1. Web-based research
      A. Objective: To increase awareness of how and when to use the World Wide Web as a research resource.
      B. Procedure: First, make sure all students have relatively easy access to the Web or make arrangements to ensure their access; have students work in teams of 2-3 to conduct research on communication concepts that would enhance their understanding. For example, credibility, persuasion, listening, speaking across diverse cultures might be topics explored. Have them develop resource lists based on their research, and report to the class the strategies they used in finding materials.
      C. Discussion: Focus part of the attention on what kinds of information/resources they uncovered that were most interesting or useful from their perspective; focus also on the kinds of strategies employed, as students will teach each other, as well as you, in conveying their electronic 'savvy.'

2. Interviewing
      A. Objective: To increase students' understanding of how effective interviewing techniques are applied.
      B. Procedure: Obtain a tape of an interview such as Face the Nation or a Barbara Walters special or ask students to watch an interview program. Students should record the primary questions and interview format. Then, they should outline the structure of the interview.
      C. Discussion: Interviews can be reported to the rest of the class and evaluated for their effectiveness in eliciting information. You may use the Interview Assessment Form included at the end of this chapter.

3. Substitute Sources
      A. Objective: To help students identify and choose appropriate forms of supporting material.
      B. Procedure: Form students in groups of 3-5. Choose a sample speech from the textbook and ask each group to identify each form of supporting material used in the speech. Members of the group should then substitute other forms of supporting material in the speech. A recorder should note all the changes and present them to the class.
      C. Discussion: Which forms of supporting material worked most effectively? Would the choice of supporting material vary with different audiences? Identify several audiences and the forms of supporting material which would work best for each.

4. Supporting Claims
      A. Objective: To link supporting material with speaker claims.

B. Procedure: List claims made by speakers in the last round of classroom speeches or ask each student to list several claims in one of their previous speeches.

C. Discussion: What supporting material was provided in the speech? What additional supporting material could have been used? Where would a speaker find that information? Considering the audience and speech purpose, which form of supporting material would be most effective?

5. Pairing Up

A. Objective: To provide feedback on supporting materials prior to the next speech assignment.

B. Procedure: Assign pairs. Provide time for each pair to review the next speech before it is given in class. Each pair should provide comments on the use of supporting material in the speech.

C. Discussion: Where would more supporting material enhance the impact of the speech? Is the variety of supporting material sufficient? Does the supporting material provide adequate evidence of the point being discussed in the speech? Is the source of the supporting material credible for this audience?

6. Additional Activities: Assign an interview as part of the search for supporting materials for the next classroom speech. Forms for planning and assessing interviews can be found at the end of this chapter. Additional exercises include: Recognition of Supporting Materials, Supporting Assertions, Citing Supporting Material, and Impact of Supporting Materials.

Impromptu Speaking Activities

1. Interview Impromptu

A. Objective: Application of guidelines for constructing and conducting a good interview.

B. Procedure: Pair students and provide each pair with a mock situation such as employer-employee interview, special presidential press conference, etc. Ask each pair to briefly determine their roles and then present them in an impromptu role-play for the class.

2. Citing Supporting Material

A. Objective: To provide students with an opportunity to practice citing supporting material orally.

B. Procedure: Hand each student one page from a recent news weekly such as Time, Newsweek, or U.S.News. Ask each student to prepare a brief informative speech using one or more facts from the page. The student should be encouraged to cite the source orally in this impromptu speech.

Additional Resources

Bowers, A. Anne. "The Television Interview." Speech Communication Teacher 7
        (1993): 4-5.

Collins, Mauri. "Internet Information Management Tools." Communication Education 43
        (1994): 112-119. (Note: This volume is devoted to the Internet.)

Grainer, Diane. "What's Evidence." Speech Communication Teacher 7 (1993): 10-11.

Kent, Michael L., "Getting the Most From Your Search Engine" Communication Teacher 15
        (2000): 4-6.

Mills, Daniel. "The Interview Fair: Maximizing Opportunity and Experience." Speech
        Communication Teacher 7 (1993): 11-12.

Reinard, John. "The Empirical Study of the Persuasive Effects of Evidence: The Status After
        Fifty Years of Research." Human Communication Research 15 (1988): 3-59.

Smith, Robert E. "Clustering: A Way to Discover Speech Topics." Speech Communication
        Teacher 7 (1993): 6-7.

Thompson, Carol. "Fantasy Interviews." Speech Communication Teacher 8 (1994): 7.

Willer, Lynda. "Learning Research Skills...and Having Fun While Doing It." Speech
        Communication Teacher 9 (1995): 12-13.

RECOGNITION OF SUPPORTING MATERIALS

Identify the following uses of evidence including testimony, comparisons, specific instances or illustrations, and explanations. Be sure to look carefully at the way the information is used in each example.

1.   For the cost of one elementary school teacher today, you could have hired 6 of them in the early 1900's.

2.   The three types of speeches are persuasive, informative, and humorous.

3.   My roommate swears by it--it really works.

4.   A college education today is worth more than $250,000 in additional income over a lifetime than is a high school education.

5.   The score is 7 to nothing at the bottom of the eighth.

6.   My annual $44,000 income is in the same range as most of my neighbors' incomes.

7.   Russia launched the Sputnik in early 1959.

8.   Aristotle saw rhetoric as "the faculty of observing, in any given case, all the available means of persuasion."

9.   Aristotle's definition of rhetoric is similar to many contemporary communication scholars' use of the term.

10.   I didn't attend my first college football game until last weekend with my parents.

11.   In the decades since the first Earth Day, the Federal government has passed more than 80 laws aimed at safeguarding air, water, land, and public health.

12.   A White House spokesperson reported that the first lady's condition is guarded after her bout with intestinal flu earlier in the week.

13.   Americans, by European standards, are extremely wasteful of precious natural resources such as oil and natural gas.

14.   BP, Mobil, and Exxon are American's largest money-making institutions outside of the Federal government itself.

15.   In order to produce a professional looking garment, the home seamstress must follow one basic rule: Press every seam before proceeding to another.

16.   In 1970 that magazine cost $.50. Today the price has gone up a whopping 125% over its earlier price.

17.   The 1989 student demonstrations in China have inspired freedom-seeking peoples world-wide.

18.   It is impossible for two parallel lines to intersect because they are following the same planes.

19.   Fidel Castro served as a hero for Cubans in the 1950's much like George Washington symbolized freedom for American colonists.

20.   Martin Luther King, Jr.'s words, "I have a dream my four little children will one day live in a nation where they will not be judged by the color of their skin but by content of their character" are still inspiring.

SUPPORTING ASSERTIONS

Decide what it would take to convince you that each of the following assertions is true. Remember, you are not asked to determine if the statement is true, but what it would take to convince you that it is true.

1.   The walls in this room are painted green.

2.   Lief Erickson sailed to the Great Lakes region in 1402.

3.   Women are better drivers than men.

4.   Former President Bill Clinton was completely innocent of any involvement in the Lewinsky scandal.

5.   Dictatorships are better for economic development than democracies.

6.   The Rev. Jimmy Swaggart is an immoral person.

7.   The United States should legalize all narcotic drugs.

8.   Teachers who publish their research are better classroom instructors.

9.   Every student on campus should be required to take an Asian history class.

10.   Wealthy people receive more justice than poor people in the American legal system.

11.   The sun sets in the East.

12.   We should abolish all speed limits on interstate highways.

13.   Britney Spears is the most gifted entertainer of our time.

14.   It is better to be 80 years old than 8 years old.

CITING SUPPORTING MATERIAL: PCIA

In order to maximize the impact of your supporting material, follow this simple formula — P-C-I-A. — it will help you maximize your supporting materials in your speech:

Preview: "More Americans are dying in alcohol-related accidents than ever before."
Cite: "According to the latest report from the Highway Safety Administration, 7 out of ten accidents involve alcohol."
Interpret: "Well over half of all accidents occurring today involve the misuse of alcohol."
Apply: "Most of us don't think about it when we drive to the store or make plans to drive home for spring break, but the odds are that we will meet a drunk driver-- head-on!"

Answer the following questions about the supporting material you plan to use in your next speech:

1.   What will you tell your listeners to expect?

2.   What special qualifications of your source make it especially credible for your audience? How will you state your source's qualifications?

3.   Do you need to paraphrase ideas or cut out unnecessary words when quoting supporting material directly?

4.   How will you summarize the most important point(s) in your supporting material after you've cited it? What will you say?

5.   How will you apply your supporting material to your audience to make the greatest impact? Can you compare it to something they're already familiar with? How will this knowledge affect them now or in the future? Can you make the impact vivid for them?

6.   Are you making the best choices of supporting material? Can you find supporting materials for which the answers to these questions show the potential for greater audience impact than the supporting material you'd planned to use?

IMPACT OF SUPPORTING MATERIALS: PCIA

Follow the same P-C-I-A process when using supporting materials in a speech. This process will maximize the impact of your supporting materials. After reviewing the process, apply it to the fictitious quotes supplied below.

P Tell your listeners what to expect. This takes advantage of selective perception or "listener set."

C Read/cite the supporting material.

I Interpret the supporting material. Provide your listeners with your interpretation of the import.

A Apply it directly to your listeners' lives. You might compare it to something they already know or explain how it will affect them now or in the future.

Here's a sample of this process:

"One recent explanation for the huge burden on taxpayers is the staggering number of unsupported children on the welfare roles. According to an article in Newsweek, June 21, 2002: "Out-of-wedlock births have exploded nationally, from 544,000 in 1990 to 1.1 million in 2000. . . "Of those, 66 percent of the fathers are never identified. In many cases, the burden for supporting their children falls heavily on the taxpayer. You and I pick up the responsibility of these absent fathers every time we pay our federal and state taxes."

Now, apply the same process to maximize the impact of supporting material in each of the following cases:

TOPIC: Shopping Online   SOURCE: Computing, July, 1999, p. 152
EVIDENCE: "Of the 56.4 million people who shopped online in the first quarter of 1999, only 23. 5 million purchased something, according to eMarketer."

TOPIC: Cuba SOURCE: Cigar Aficionado, June, 1999, p. 111.
EVIDENCE: "When the Soviet empire began to collapse in 1989, so did Cuba's economy."

TOPIC: Cuba SOURCE: Cigar Aficionado, June, 1999, p. 87; article by Sen. Christopher Dodd advocating an end to the embargo (companion article by Sen. Jesse Helms argues against ending the embargo).
EVIDENCE: "Our policy has been one that denies food to hungry Cuban children; that severely limits the availability of medicines and medical supplies to the Cuban people;. . . . in short, it is a policy that is inconsistent with America's values and self interests."

TOPIC: Online Auctions   SOURCE: Yahoo, June, 1999, p. 80.
EVIDENCE: "Jupiter Communications estimates that by 2002, there will be 6.5 million bidders (up from 1.2 million in 1998) spending $ 3.2 billion a year at online auctions."

INTERVIEW PLANNING FORM

I. INTERVIEW OBJECTIVES:
   A. What are your primary objectives?

   B. What is the general purpose of this interview?

   C. What is your role in this interview?

   D. What will be the expectations of the other participant(s)?

II. SPECIAL PREPARATION:
   A. Will you need to do any specific research prior to this interview? If so, explain.

   B. Will you need notes? a tape recorder? special documents? other aids?

   C. What arrangements should be made for the interview time and place?

III. INTERVIEW QUESTIONS:
   A. Which primary questions will you ask?

   B. Which direct and indirect questions will you ask?

   C. Which open and closed questions will you ask?

IV. INTERVIEW FOLLOW-UP:
   A. On what note will you close the interview?

   B. What action will you take following the interview?

INTERVIEW ASSESSMENT FORM	GOOD	ADEQUATE	POOR
INTERVIEW PLANNING			
1. Clearly Structured			
2. Mutually recognized goals			
3. Clear Purpose			
4. Role specific			
INTERVIEW QUESTIONS			
1. Planned well			
2. Organized effectively			
3. Appropriate			
4. Varied			
5. Adequately blended			
COMMUNICATION SKILLS			
1. Effective listening			
2. Builds rapport			
3. Clearly phrased statements			
4. Interactive (turn-taking			

Summary of Evaluation:

CHAPTER 7.   STRUCTURING THE SPEECH: LANGUAGE DEVICES, INTERNAL ORGANIZATION PACKAGES, AND THE MOTIVATED SEQUENCE

CHAPTER CONTENT

Micro-Structures: Using Language to Organize Ideas
Meso-Structures: Patterns of Internal Organization
     Chronological Patterns
     Spatial Patterns
     Causal Patterns
     Topical Patterns
     How to Choose from among Meso-Structures
Macro-Structure: The Five Basic Steps of the Motivated Sequence
     The Attention Step
     The Need Step
     The Satisfaction Step
     The Visualization Step
     The Action Step
Using the Motivated Sequence to Frame A Speech
     Framing the Speech to Inform
     Framing the Speech to Persuade
     Framing the Speech to Actuate
     Framing the Speech to Entertain
Assessing a Sample Speech: Drug Testing: Outcome, Death by Justin Neal
Integrating Meso-Structures into the Motivated Sequence
Chapter Summary
Key Terms
Assessment Activities
References

Discussion Questions

1. What is the difference between micro, meso and macro-structures?
2. Explain the natural tendency to organize information in order to interpret it. How does language help us to organize information?
3. What are some language strategies you use for organizing parts of your life?
4. What are the 5 basic steps in the motivated sequence?
5. Read the speech by Maria Lucia R. Anton in your textbook. Identify each of the steps of Monroe's Motivated Sequence in the speech.
6. What is the purpose of the satisfaction step?
7. What is included in the satisfaction step in the speech to inform?
8. Give an example of the satisfaction step for a speech to inform (to persuade or to actuate, to entertain).
9. How does the satisfaction step in the speech to entertain differ from the speech to inform? from the speech to persuade or actuate?
10. What is the function of the visualization step? Provide an example of it.
11. What is the positive method of visualization? the negative method? the contrast method?
12. How should the action step be developed in a speech to actuate? to persuade? to inform? to entertain?
13. What are the five key criteria to keep in mind while you organize your speech using Monroe's Motivated Sequence?
14. What is the defining characteristic of a chronological pattern of organization? temporal sequence? narrative sequence? spatial pattern? causal pattern?
15. Give an example of a speech topic that would be best organized using the chronological pattern (temporal sequence, narrative sequence, spatial pattern, causal pattern?
16. Explain the difference between cause-effect pattern and effect-cause pattern. Use an example for each.
17. When should you use a cause-effect sequence to organize your speech? effect-cause?
18. When are topical patterns of organization useful?
19. What is the relationship between the motivated sequence and the chronological, spatial, causal, and topical patterns?

Questions to Stimulate Critical Thinking

1. Several scholars have observed that mass media, particularly television, have altered the way people organize their thoughts. What impact do you think media has had on human thinking?
2. How do you think patterns of organization are learned?
3. Are patterns of organization related to human thought processes? If so, how?
4. How is structure both psychological and logical?

5. Recall the organization of your last speech. Can you imagine the main points occurring in a different order? What impact would the rearrangement have on the effect of the speech?

6. Consider the current trends in television advertisements. Do they rely on a particular organizational pattern? Has this pattern changed over the past several years?

7. To what extent does culture have an impact on the ways people organize ideas? How has your culture affected your ability to organize?

8. Can you think of instances when the steps of the motivated sequence might be rearranged to enhance the impact on listeners? Defend your examples.

9. Recall the plot of your favorite novel, film, or television episode. Can you discover the organizational pattern inherent in it? What would happen if you rearranged the events? What impact do you think this reorganization would have on its effect?

10. Do you think the pattern of organization a speaker chooses affects the delivery of the speech? the kind of introduction or conclusion chosen? the kinds of supporting material used? the audience response?

11. What elements of demographic or psychological audience analysis might affect the organizational pattern chosen by a speaker?

Application Exercises

1. Organizing to Speak

A. Objective: To apply the concept of varied organizational patterns to speech topics and purposes.

B. Procedure: Divide the chalkboard into three columns, labeling for speaking to inform, persuade/actuate and entertain. Ask students for sample topics under each category of speech purpose in a short brainstorming session. Then, choosing one or more topics from each category of speech purpose, ask for the best pattern of organization for the topic.

C. Discussion: Probe for students' understanding of how patterns of organization are influenced by the audience, occasion, topic, and purpose of the speech. If several patterns of organization appear possible, discuss the strengths and weaknesses of each choice. Use the Patterns of Organization form at the end of this chapter to follow up this exercise.

2. Linking Ideas

A. Objective: To help students connect outlining with clarity of thought.

B. Procedure: Ask students to bring in copies of their next speech in outline form with each full sentence on a separate strip of paper. Pair students and ask that they exchange outlines after each has scrambled the outline. Then, each student is to reconstruct the outline in its most logical pattern. When students have finished reconstructing the outlines, they should check for accuracy with the original organization.

C. Discussion: Students should ascertain whether their speech outlines are relatively easy for others to follow and how well their ideas are communicated by their patterns of organization.

3. Perspectives on a Film

A. Objective: To illustrate the potential for using various types of organization and guide students as they experiment with different organizational patterns.

B. Procedure: After discussing the principles of outlining and the types of organization, divide students into four groups. Choose a film that most, if not all, students have seen. The original Star Wars film often works well for this exercise. Assign each group an organizational pattern and focus for development. After each group has finished the exercise, ask a group member to report to the class on the results of their task. Note: For a variation of this exercise, assign each group the same organizational pattern but a different focus. For the Star Wars film, the following patterns can be assigned:

Topical Pattern--focus on the main characters, the heroes/villains, the various kinds of droids, the special effects, etc.

Chronological Pattern--outline the plot of the movie

Spatial Pattern--outline the places where action occurs, the layout of the Death Star, the interior of the Millennium Falcon, the appearance of R2-D2, etc.

Cause-Effect Pattern--focus on the reasons for the emergence of the resistance, the reasons for various characters' behaviors, the interaction between characters such as Darth Vader and Ben Kinobe

C. Discussion: What are the results of each groups' analysis? How do the outcomes differ? What accounts for the difference in outlines? What pattern of organization was used in each case? How do we know that pattern was used? What would result if another pattern of organization were used instead?

4. Sample Speech Exercise

A. Objective: To apply the motivated sequence to speech preparation and evaluation.

B. Procedure: After reading the sample speech provided in the chapter, ask students to identify the steps of the motivated sequence and evaluate how effectively each step is developed by the speaker.

C. Discussion: What options does the speaker have in preparing a speech using the motivated sequence?

5. Adapting the Motivated Sequence to the Speech Purpose

A. Objective: To develop the students' sophistication in adapting the motivated sequence to the purpose of the speech.

B. Procedure: Assign four groups and ask each group to choose a topic. Then, following the steps of the motivated sequence, require each group to plan a speech for one of the general purposes of speaking.

C. Discussion: How does actual implementation of the   motivated sequence vary from one kind of speech to another?

6. Other exercises: See "Reconstructing a Speech" later in this Chapter.

Impromptu Speaking Activities

1. Sales Talks
   A. Objective: Implementation of the motivated sequence.
   B. Procedure: Give students several minutes to invent a product and plan a commercial for the product. Ask each student to present the commercial using the motivated sequence to organize the impromptu speech.

2. Group Speech
   A. Objective: Planning a step of the motivated sequence.
   B. Procedure: Assign students to 5 groups and provide each group with one of the steps of the motivated sequence. Write a product, an idea, or a speech topic and purpose on the chalkboard and give each group several minutes to develop the step it has been assigned. Ask someone from the group to present the groups' ideas to the rest of the class. If the steps are presented in order, a rough draft of a speech should emerge.

3. Cooperative Sequencing
   A. Objective: To simulate a speech organized using the motivated sequence.
   B. Procedure: Announce a topic for a speech to actuate. Use a topic(s) with which students have some familiarity. Draw a name or designate a student to deliver the attention step of the speech and continue with the remaining four steps asking one student to develop each step of the motivated sequence. At the conclusion of this "speech" suggest additional topics and continue with impromptu speakers completing additional speeches.

4. Organizing Your Speech
   A. Objective: To increase students' awareness of the role of patterns of organization in speaking.
   B. Procedure: Ask students to draw cards on which impromptu topics and a pattern of organization have been printed. They should develop the ideas on the topic in the pattern of organization indicated.

5. Linking Supporting Materials and Organization
   A. Objective: To provide practice in organizing an impromptu speech while using effective supporting materials.

B. Procedure: Provide students with one of the quotations from Linking Supporting Materials and Organization form at the end of this chapter. Ask each student to explain what the quotation means in an impromptu speech. Students should use previews, summaries, and transitions to organize their speeches as well as several forms of supporting materials to amplify their explanations.

Additional Resources

Dolphin, Carol Zinner, "Using the Monroe Motivated Sequence: A Group Exercise," <u>Speech Communication Teacher</u> 11 (1997):12.

Mino, Mary. "Structuring: An Alternate Approach for Developing Class Organization." <u>Speech Communication Teacher</u> 5 (1991): 14-15.

PATTERNS OF ORGANIZATION

Identify the pattern of organization that would be best for each of the following speech topics:

_____	1. how a gasoline engine runs
_____	2. why we entered WWII
_____	3. children's acquisition of language
_____	4. understanding AIDS (Acquired Immuno-Deficiency Syndrome)
_____	5. the rise & fall of the Roman Empire
_____	6. migration patterns of Canadian geese
_____	7. using your college library
_____	8. my summer vacation
_____	9. events that lead up to the siege of the Alamo
_____	10. the life of Elizabeth Taylor
_____	11. common garden herbs
_____	12. amazing human feats
_____	13. fasten your seatbelt
_____	14. the discovery of the source of the Nile river
_____	15. how the movie "Matrix" was filmed
_____	16. touring the National Gallery of Art
_____	17. using earth tones to decorate your home
_____	18. the story of Shrek's creation
_____	19. sign your organ donor card
_____	20. musical highlights of American operettas
_____	21. the symptoms of diabetes
_____	22. how to study for the SAT examination
_____	23. recent advances in psychiatry
_____	24. the process of brewing beer
_____	25. the design of Epcot Center
_____	26. popular summer holidays
_____	27. the Battle of Gettysburg
_____	28. Japanese inventors
_____	29. how to make money in the stock market
_____	30. chess

LINKING SUPPORTING MATERIALS AND ORGANIZATION

Draw a quotation, then in a short impromptu speech, explain what it means. Use a clear preview, specific transitions, and a short summary. Supporting material should be added to amplify the explanation--examples, statistics, testimony, etc.

The race is not alone to the swift.

A long dispute means that both parties are wrong.

A rolling stone gathers no moss.

Don't swap horses in the middle of a stream.

None so blind as those who will not see.

No answer is also an answer.

Necessity is the mother if invention.

A barber learns to shave by shaving fools.

A bird in the hand is worth two in the bush.

You can't steal second with one foot on first.

A drowning person will catch at a straw.

A good beginning is half the battle.

A light purse makes a heavy heart.

A miss is as good as a mile.

All is not gold that glistens.

We do what we must, and call it by the best names.

An open door may tempt a saint.

Every man, deep down, is a fisherman.

Birds of a feather flock together.

Brevity is the soul of wit.

Don't burn your house to scare the mice.

Do not keep a dog and bark yourself.

Every horse thinks its own load heaviest.

Friends are a second existence.

When one is up to the neck in alligators, it is difficult to realize that the original purpose was just to drain the swamp.

Success has ruined many a person.

To teach is to learn twice.

EVALUATION FORM: MOTIVATED SEQUENCE

Name _____ Topic _____

Speaking Time _____

ORGANIZATION

I. **Attention Step**: Clear, stated emphatically
   actually creates a need to listen

_____

II. **Need Step**: Clear well defined problem
   area, supported by adequate example/evidence,
   ramifications outlined and related to audience

_____

III. **Satisfaction Step**: Adequate statement of solution,
   proof of practicality and desirability of solution,
   demonstrated solution meets need, examples of
   solution applied, answered potential objections,
   audience involved

_____

IV. **Visualization Step**: Clearly result of solution,
   advantages drawn, problems if solution not adopted,
   future conditions pictured, varied motivational
   appeals employed

_____

V. **Call for Action**: Summarized problem and solution,
   clear action requested, heightened audience
   involvement, final statement reinforced

_____

DELIVERY
 Enthusiastic, adequate eye contact, limited
  use of notes, purposeful gestures and bodily
  movement, fluent vocal delivery, energetic,
  appropriate vocal and physical reinforcement,
  appearance of involvement, sincere

_____

OVERALL IMPRESSION
 Sincere, credible, charismatic, created need
 to act in accordance with speech purpose

MONROE'S MOTIVATED SEQUENCE IN THE MEDIA

Attach a print ad to this page from a popular magazine. Identify each step of Monroe's Motivated sequence as it occurs verbally or visually in your advertisement.

STEP	VERBAL	VISUAL
1. ATTENTION		
2. NEED		
3. SATISFACTION		
4. VISUALIZATION		
5. ACTION		

EVALUATING THE MOTIVATED SEQUENCE

<u>Ratings</u> 5 = excellent 4 = good 3 = average 2 = fair 1 = poor

---

<u>Attention Step</u>
     created audience interest   _____
     introduced speech topic   _____
     previewed main ideas   _____
     created desire to listen   _____

<u>Need Step</u>
     developed need thoroughly   _____
     used adequate support   _____
     appealed to motivations   _____

<u>Satisfaction Step</u>
     developed adequate plan   _____
     plan adapted to need   _____
     practicality demonstrated   _____

<u>Visualization Step</u>
     related to listeners   _____
     impact developed clearly   _____
     adequate imagery used   _____

<u>Action Step</u>
     specific action developed   _____
     audience involved   _____
     strong appeal used   _____

<u>Overall Use</u>
     appropriateness of steps   _____
     internally structured   _____
     overall coherence   _____

CHAPTER 8.   MAINTAINING AUDIENCE ATTENTION AND INVOLVEMENT

CHAPTER CONTENT

Chapter Summary
Key Terms
Assessment Activities
References

Discussion Questions

1. What is attention?
2. What are the nine factors of attention? Provide an example of each.
3. What advice would you give to a speaker who decides to use humor during a speech?
4. How can you communicate self-confidence while speaking?
5. What are important considerations to make while you are evaluating the speeches of others?
6. How is introducing and concluding a speech like framing a new house?
7. What is rhetorical orientation and how does understanding this concept assist in framing a speech?
8. What are the three purposes of well-prepared introductions?
9. What is a forecast? Provide an example. How does it help orient listeners?
10. What initial considerations must a speaker make about the audience before determining the kind of introduction for a speech?
11. As a speaker, how can you enhance your credibility in an introduction?
12. Identify the various methods for introducing a speech. Provide an example of each.
13. How can a speaker integrate audience expectations and demands of the occasion in a speech introduction?
14. When is a personal greeting especially effective as an introduction?
15. What is the advantage of asking a question to begin the speech?
16. When should a speaker startle the audience in an introduction?
17. How does an introductory quotation focus attention on the speech topic?
18. What three communication rules should govern the use of humor in an introduction?
19. When should a speaker use an illustration to open a speech?
20. What are the functions of a speech conclusion?
21. How can a speaker successfully signal the conclusion of a speech? Why is it important to do so?
22. Identify the methods of concluding a speech suggested by your text.
23. What are the advantages of summarizing your major points or ideas in your conclusion?
24. Under what circumstances is the speaker's statement of personal intention particularly effective as a concluding device?

Questions to Stimulate Critical Thinking

1. Explain which of the nine factors of attention may stimulate greater audience attention than the others. Be ready to defend your choices.
2. Randomly choose a speech topic. For a speech on this topic, identify how each of the nine factors of attention could be used to stimulate audience attention.
3. For your favorite television program, identify how each of the nine factors of attention is used to hold audience attention.
4. Make a list of your favorite films. How is each 'framed,' that is, introduced and concluded? How does the frame set up viewer expectations and achieve closure?
5. Investigate the concepts of primacy and recency. How do these concepts apply to events like meeting new people, competing in horse shows, or selecting the evening line-up of television shows?
6. How can the factors of attention aid the speaker in finding a creative and attention-gaining introduction for a speech?
7. Is there a difference between a quotation used for proof and a quotation used as an introductory device? If so, what is it?
8. What criteria should be used for a carefully selected introductory quotation?
9. Investigate the concept of selective perception. How does a speech introduction influence listeners' perceptions? How does a forecast focus listeners' attention?
10. When should a speaker combine the different forms of introductions or conclusions? Provide an example of combined introduction or conclusion.
11. Imagine yourself confronted by a group of listeners who are vitally interested in your speech topic but who are also initially very hostile to your position on the topic. In addition, your credibility on this topic is very low. What kind of introduction should you prepare? Justify your answer.
12. If you were selected to write speeches for the President of the United States, what would you have to consider when preparing the President's speech introductions and conclusions?
13. Think about your favorite speech. How does the speaker introduce (conclude) the speech? What makes the introduction (conclusion) particularly effective?

Application Exercises

1. Applying the Factors of Attention
   A. Objective: To provide the student with practical experience in adapting the factors of attention.
   B. Procedure: Using a sample speech from the text, a speech provided by the instructor, or a speech from the previous round of student speaking, identify the factors of attention actually used in the speech. Then, ask the class to provide alternative ways to gain or maintain attention working within the framework of the original speech.

C. Discussion: Compare the options a speaker has for gaining and maintaining attention. Discuss the best choices for the speaker among the factors of attention in view of the speaker's purpose, audience, and occasion.

2. Examining the Nightly News
   A. Objective: To reveal how informative speakers such as newscasters employ the factors of attention to hold viewer interest.
   B. Procedure: Tape a television newscast and replay it during the class period. Ask each student to write down as many factors of attention as he/she notices during the newscast.
   C. Discussion: Which factors of attention were used? Were any of the factors of attention used more frequently than others? Why or why not? To what extent does the newscaster influence audience attentiveness by framing information for greatest impact?

3. Adapting Introductions and Conclusions
   A. Objective: To reinforce the student's understanding that it is possible to introduce or conclude a speech in several different ways, depending upon variables such as audience and occasion.
   B. Procedure: Using one or several of the example speeches from the textbook, ask students to create a different introduction and conclusion for the speech. In each case, you may vary the audience, occasion, and purpose of the speech. Write an appropriate introduction and conclusion for the altered situation.
   C. Discussion: What variables of the speaking situation make demands upon a speaker? How can each of these be taken into account in the introduction and conclusion? Can a speech "succeed" or "fail" because of its introduction and conclusion?

4. Revising Introductions and Conclusions
   A. Objective: To offer students an opportunity to revise the introduction and conclusion to a speech and assess its impact.
   B. Procedure: Ask students to change the introduction and conclusion to a previous speech they have given. The speech can be one which was ineffective or it can be a speech for which the focus has changed. Ask students to present the new introduction and conclusion (the body of the speech should be omitted to save time).
   C. Discussion: In each case, do the altered introduction and conclusion achieve the intended purposes? Under what circumstances would the former introduction and conclusion be more effective? Are there other ideas which the speaker might use to introduce or conclude this speech?

5. Developing a Rhetorical Orientation

    A. Objective: To provide practice in developing a rhetorical orientation.

    B. Procedure: Brainstorm for speech purposes, situations, and audiences. List the results on the chalkboard. Ask students to develop an effective introduction and conclusion for one of the speeches listed. You might start the brainstorming by suggesting the following examples:

        1. A speech honoring the winner of the local Special Olympics delivered at a banquet attended by the contestants and their parents

        2. A speech to solicit organ donors at a church group meeting

        3. A eulogy for a distant relative given to family members

        4. A speech to actuate that is presented at a union meeting where a strike vote will be taken

        5. An announcement of impending layoffs at a gathering of local manufacturing plant employees

    C. Discussion: Which introductions and conclusions seem most appropriate in each case? Why? How does the audience affect your choice of introduction and conclusion? What effect does the situation have on choosing an appropriate introduction and conclusion? What would be inappropriate choices in each case?

6. Reaching Closure

    A. Objective: To encourage observation of the functions of conclusions in classroom settings.

    B. Procedure: Conduct an experiment. For one week, require that each student record how their instructors signal the conclusion of classes. They should note in writing what was said at the end of each class session.

    C. Discussion: Compare the findings. What is the most common method of concluding classes? What is the most effective way that instructors conclude class sessions? What purposes does the conclusion to a class session serve? What similarities exist between concluding a class and concluding a speech?

7. Forecasting

    A. Objective: To focus attention on the role of forecasting in a speech introduction.

    B. Procedure: Prior to the next speech assignment, ask each student to bring their preliminary speech outline to class. Share each outline, then suggest ways the speaker can forecast the main ideas of the speech.

    C. Discussion: What is the best way to phrase the forecast? How many ideas should be forecast? How detailed should the speaker make the forecast? What is the function of the forecast for the listener?

8. Additional Exercises: Assign groups to develop an introduction and conclusion for the speech on tattoos provided in the worksheet at the end of this chapter. Also, have students use the two REVIEW sheets for Introducing and Concluding a Speech at the end of this Chapter.

Impromptu Speaking Activities

1. Duets
    A. Objective: To provide students with an opportunity to practice delivering introductions and conclusions and also to stress the coordination of the introduction and the conclusion.
    B. Procedure: Assign partners and ask each pair to write an introduction and a conclusion to a fictitious speech (the speech topic can be determined by the pair or you can assign one or two general topic areas for the entire group). Each pair should keep in mind that the introduction and conclusion should reflect the same focus and speaker purpose. Ask each student to deliver either the introduction or conclusion to the fictitious speech.

2. Introduction (or Conclusion) Chain
    A. Objective: To encourage creative ways to introduce (or conclude) speeches.
    B. Procedure: Briefly review the kinds of introductions (or conclusions) and their purposes. Explain the process and begin: Everyone holds their hand in the air until they have been called upon or the process starts over. One student begins by calling out a topic (such as cooking, library books, chemistry, aviation, etc.) and calls upon a student whose hand is raised. That student can put his or her hand down after providing a quick introduction (or conclusion) or idea for one. The chain continues as each student who participates calls upon someone else whose hand is raised until all hands are down. This exercise can be conducted quite rapidly once students understand it.

3. Developing Credibility
    A. Objective: To encourage students to use introductions to enhance their credibility in speeches.
    B. Procedure: Ask each student to think of a topic on which they consider themselves experts (or highly credible). After giving them a few minutes to think about their credibility, ask each student to present a quick introduction to a speech in which they develop their credibility on the topic.

Additional Resources

Magee, Mary and Melinda Davies. "Crafting a Powerhouse Introduction." Training and
    Development Journal 43 (1989): 25-27.
Overton, J. "Introductions and Conclusions: Helping Public Speaking Students Write Effective
    Beginnings and Endings." Speech Communication Teacher 9 (1994): 4.
Walter, S. "Introduction of a Speaker: Multipurpose and Multicultural." Speech
    Communication Teacher 9 (1994): 3.

DEVELOPING AN INTRODUCTION AND CONCLUSION

The following outline is for a speech to inform on the topic of tattoos. Develop an appropriate introduction and conclusion for the speech.

<u>Your Introduction</u>:

I.   A brief history of tattoos
    A.   Prehistoric records of scarring of human skin
    B.   Tattoos often considered rite of passage into adulthood
    C.   Trade brought Europeans into contact with the practice of tattooing
    D.   Tattooing spread throughout Europe after contact with other cultures
    E.   Tattooing was outlawed in America and Europe in the 19th century
    F.   Currently tattooing is becoming popular among adolescents and women

II.   Motivations for tattooing
    A.   Tattoos stand out as unique identification
    B.   Many tattoos are considered works of art
        1.   Collectors preserve tattooed skin
        2.   Delicate colors and lines distinguish art
    C.   Tattoos also signal rebellion
        1.   Historically used in political or social dissent
        2.   Sometimes identified with criminal element

III.   The Method
    A.   An outline of the design is drawn in ink
    B.   Color is applied
        1.   Series of gouges or needle pricks push color under the skin
        2.   Process is repeated until desired color and lines achieved
    C.   Healing
        1.   Local inflammation occurs
        2.   Scabs form
        3.   Severe itching follows
        4.   Some designs require up to a year to complete and heal

<u>Your Conclusion</u>:

REVIEW: QUESTIONS FOR BEGINNING MY SPEECH

Name_____

1. Is my audience likely to be interested in my topic or must I arouse interest? How do I plan to involve my listeners?

2. Is my audience sufficiently aware of my qualifications or should I establish my expertise? How can I do so without appearing overly humble or offending my listeners?

3. Does my speech fulfill or depart from the expectations of the audience or occasion? Should I clarify my reasons for the purpose or direction of my speech?

4. Do I need to create an atmosphere of good will? How can I begin to do so early in the speech?

5. How much prior knowledge do my listeners have of my topic?

6. How can I forecast the major points of my speech clearly for my listeners?

7. Given all of these responses, what is the best way to introduce my speech?

REVIEW: QUESTIONS FOR CONCLUDING MY SPEECH

Name_____

1.   What do I plan to say to signal that I am concluding my speech?

2.   Do I need a summary of my main points to reinforce them for my listeners?

3.   How can I tie the ideas of my speech directly into my listeners' vital interests and concerns?

4.   What mood or tone do I intend to create as I conclude my speech?

5.   How do I intend to reach closure as I end my speech? Can I refer back to an introductory scenario or question? Is there another way I can come full circle in my conclusion?

6.   Do I want my listeners to act on the ideas or information in my speech? How do I intend to reinforce that action in my conclusion?

7.   Is my conclusion intended to inspire listeners? If so, what images or language choices can I make to create that inspiration?

CHAPTER 9.   DEVELOPING THE SPEECH OUTLINE

CHAPTER CONTENT

Requirements of Good Outline Form
  Communication Research Dateline: The Organization of Subordinate Points
Developing the Speech: Stages in the Outlining Process
  Developing a Rough Outline
  Developing a Technical Plot Outline
  Developing a Speaking Outline
  Using PowerPoint to Integrate Verbal and Visual Outlines
Chapter Summary
Key Terms
Assessment Activities
References

Discussion Questions

1.   Why do speakers need outlines?
2.   What are the requirements of good outline form? Provide an example of each.
3.   Why is it important that each item in an outline contain only one unit of information?
4.   Why is proper subordination of main points and subpoints important to the total purpose of the speech?
5.   Why should proper symbols and proper indentation be used in an outline?
6.   What additional requirement applies to the final draft of a formal outline?
7.   What are the stages of outlining?
8.   What is a rough outline? What does one look like (provide example)?
9.   What is a technical plot outline? What is its purpose?
10.   What is a speaking outline?
11.   How does a speaking outline differ from a technical plot outline?
12.   How might PowerPoint be used to integrate visual and verbal material?

Questions to Stimulate Critical Thinking

1.   Do you think that outlining your ideas for a speech can sometimes stifle your creativity?

2.   What alternatives to outlining can you think of for organizing a speech?

3.   Consider other methods of indicating relationships such as tree diagrams or organization flow charts. What do these methods have in common with outlining? What is different?

4.   Is the urge to organize or create order an innate human need? Why or why not?

5.   Consider stand-up comedy routines which are often loosely organized. How does the comedian introduce a sense of order for the audience?

6.   As a listener, how important is it for you to understand the order of the topics a speaker will address? Are you similar or different from others in your class?

7.   Are there instances when organization or order are counterproductive? If so, when?

8.   What is the best format for your speaking notes?

9.   Sometimes students claim that they write an outline only after they have prepared their speeches. Do you think this is a good idea? Why or why not?

10.   Some research indicates that good organization enhances a speaker's credibility. What do you think is the relationship between organization and credibility?

Application Exercises

1. Scrambled Outlines
   A. Objective: To provide students with hands-on experience in organizing speeches
   B. Procedure: Ask each student to write out the outline for their last speaking assignment, writing one main item from the outline on a separate card or section of paper. Each student should then scramble the cards so that the organization of the points in the speech is no longer clear. Assign pairs and exchange scrambled speech outlines. Each student should then try to assemble the speech in a logical, well organized manner. You may allow students to help each other or introduce a competitive atmosphere by making the goal to complete the outline in the shortest time.
   C. Discussion: What distinguishes major from subpoints in an outline? What are the characteristics of each of the traditional organizational patterns? Did anything in the speech help clarify the pattern used? Does this influence the comprehension of the listener? Was the re-assembled outline clearer or more logically organized than the original? If so, why?

2. Group Outline
   A. Objective: Understanding the form and structure of the typical outline.
   B. Procedure: Provide the class with a speech topic and purpose or choose to re-write a topic from the preceding round of speeches. Use brainstorming to create the ideas which will be developed in this speech and list each on the chalkboard. Then, assemble the ideas into main ideas with subpoints according to the pattern of organization which the class deems most appropriate for the speech purpose and topic.
   C. Discussion: Determine how speakers assemble and develop their ideas and what options are available to the speaker. Use the sample outlines at the end of this chapter to develop the discussion.

3. Showing Your Notes

    A. Objective: To expose students to the kinds of speaking notes used in their speeches.

    B. Procedure: Ask each student to bring in their notecards for a major speaking assignment. Note the format of the notecards and discuss the usefulness of various speaking notes to the public speaker.

    C. Discussion: How do speaking notes influence the speaker's delivery of the message? How do speaking notes develop from the speaker's rough, full-sentence, and technical outlines?

4. Rapid Rough Outlines

    A. Objective: To reinforce the skills of developing rough outlines.

    B. Procedure: Pair students and announce a general speech topic such as "automobiles" or "dental hygiene." Give pairs two minutes to develop a rough outline for a speech on the topic. Use an overhead projector to share the results.

    C. Discussion: What primary ideas are contained in a rough outline? What organizational patterns were used in each rough outline? What is the function of the rough outline? What is the next step in developing a speech from the rough outline?

5. Developing a Technical Plot Outline

    A. Objective: To provide practice in using a technical plot outline.

    B. Procedure: Bring a videotape of a cooking, sewing, or carpentry show to class. Play the tape and ask students to note what visual aids and special effects are used. Develop a technical plot outline of the show, including each of the visual aids and special effects.

    C. Discussion: What is the purpose of a technical plot outline? When is it most useful? How can a speaker use a technical plot outline? In what other situations would a technical plot outline be important?

6. Additional exercises: Ask students to complete the Outlining Worksheet. (Provided with permission from Professor Carl Thameling, Miami University-Hamilton). Also, examine the speaking outline provided at the end of this chapter. Use the assessment form to evaluate speech outlines.

Impromptu Speaking Activities

1. Analyzing the Speech

    A. Objective: To further reinforce students' ability to recognize and choose patterns of organization.

    B. Procedure: Ask students to draw topics which have been printed on 3x5 cards. Each student should consider the various ways of developing each topic and choose which is the best pattern of organization. Ask each student to briefly explain the speaker's options and justify the choice of one as the best pattern of organization in an impromptu speech.

2. Selecting Patterns

    A. Objective: To reinforce the idea that some topics suggest their own organizational pattern.

    B. Procedure: Come to class with a list of topics that students will recognize and ask them to call out the organizational pattern that each might best utilize. Sample topics include:

        1. The Persian Gulf War – chronology, cause/effect

        2. The Grand Canyon – spatial

        3. Preparing a Resume – chronology, spatial

        4. Gaining confidence as a speaker – topical

Additional Resources

Gschwend, L. "Outlining Relay." Speech Communication Teacher 10 (1995): 9-10.

Gullickson-Tolman, Lisa, "Creating Outlines." Speech Communication Teacher 13 (1999): 7-8.

OUTLINING WORKSHEET

Directions: Circle the point that violates the principles of good outlining. Explain what is incorrect.

I.   There are many benefits to wearing seatbelts.
    A.   Seatbelts prevent passengers from being thrown around the vehicle during a collision.
    B.   Seatbelts are standard equipment in all vehicles.
    C.   Seatbelts prevent front-seat passengers from hitting the dashboard and windshield.

What is wrong with this outline?

I.   College students are classified by their academic year.
    A.   College students with fewer than 40 hours of earned credit are classified as first year students.
    B.   Sophomores are college students with more than 40 hours but fewer than 80 hours of earned credit.
    C.   Instructors who teach more than 12 hours are classified as full-time faculty members.
    D.   It takes 120 hours of earned credit to graduate from college.

What is wrong with this outline?

I.   There are more than 200 flavors of ice cream.
    A.   Frozen yogurt differs from ice cream in composition.
    B.   Strawberry is the most frequently requested flavor.
    C.   Frozen desserts are popular in the United States.

What is wrong with this outline?

I.   There are many sports featured in the summer Olympic Games.
    A.   Stadium jumping is one of the most challenging equestrian events.
    B.   Field hockey is growing in popularity.
II.   The summer Olympic Games draw international contestants.

    A.   Archery was included in the original Greek games.

    B.   Diving is an intensely competitive event.

III.   Countries hosting the summer Olympic Games have offered some of the world's most beautiful scenery.

What is wrong with this outline?

I.   More money will flow into the economy.

II.   The prime lending rate should be lowered.

III.   Housing starts will increase.

What is wrong with this outline?

I.   Dolls from the mid-twentieth century are fetching high prices from collectors.

    a.   Original Barbies command prices of $4,000 and higher.

    b.   Limited editions like Betsy McCall sell for $5,000.

    c.   G.I. Joe and Ken are selling for $2,500 to $3,500.

What is wrong with this outline?

I.   Preparing lasagna can be easy.

    A.   Bake for one hour.

    B.   Layer cooked noodles with cheeses and tomato sauce.

        1.   Alternate Swiss with Mozzarella cheese.

        2.   Lightly sprinkle oregano and basil on each layer.

    C.   Preheat the oven to 350 degrees.

What is wrong with this outline?

SAMPLE SPEAKING OUTLINE

I.   Introduction
        --Angie
        --1 million runaways <u>Health & Human Services</u>
        --15 years old
        --preview major topics

II.   Disintegration of family structure
        A.   Safety
                --36% abused <u>Psychology Today</u>
                --can't find help
        B.   React by leaving
                --short term <u>definition & examples</u>
                --long term <u>definition & example of Todd</u>

III.   More can be done
        A.   Legal changes
                --criminal laws
                --foster care
        B.   Shelters
                --only 1/2 return home
                --shelter = alternative <u>statistics & June Bucy</u>

IV.   Conclusion
        --affects us
        --solutions

ASSESSING YOUR SPEECH OUTLINE

Use the following checklist to help you evaluate your outline:

1. COMPLETENESS

    Is the outline adequately filled in?
    Are the major topic areas developed?
    Are an introduction and conclusion included?

2. PURPOSE

    Is the purpose of the speech clear?
    Is the stated purpose <u>really</u> the speech purpose? (or is this a speech to entertain in disguise, etc.)
    Does it meet the assignment?
    Can it be easily grasped by a listener?

3. STRUCTURE

    Is the speech too complex?
    Is it too simplistic?
    Is there a natural/logical progression of ideas?
    Would re-arrangement of the areas improve the flow of the speech?

4. INTRODUCTION

    Does it capture attention?
    Is it motivating?
    Does it indicate what will follow?
    Does it develop your credibility?

5. CONCLUSION

    Does it summarize main points?
    Is it too drawn out? Too abrupt?
    Is it interesting?
    Does it make a good final impression?

6. ADDITIONAL

    Do you include any special requirements such as bibliography, visual aids?
    Will the outline be handed in on time?

RECASTING THE SPEECH

Instructor: Give students duplicated copies of the scrambled outline. Form groups of four to five students. Each group should be allowed 10 to 15 minutes to agree upon and place the concepts in the proper order. One way to do this is to use Outline Symbols (I, A, 1.) -- write the appropriate symbol in front of each statement.

The objective is to gain experience linking the concepts of outline form to actual public speaking

Using the following scrambled outline -- three of the statements belong in the introduction and two in the conclusion; the remainder of the statements belong in the body of the speech --- re-order so as to construct a coherent presentation.

Outline Statements:

What are these four miracles of contemporary American suburban architecture?

The crackerbox reborn lives on as the contemporary American "ranch."

The lower level of the raised ranch, which peers out of half windows at the ground which hugs its waist, is normally used for play or work.

As a student of architecture, I have noted that suburbia has changed: your home is now reproduced not next door, but four whole gloriously different doors away.

The ranch home has three bedrooms.

In the years following World War II, the emerging suburbs of America consisted of tidy rows of crackerbox houses that differed only in the brick-a-brack that adorned them.

The middle level of the "tri" is for LDK.

The first level of the two story house is LDK and half bath.

The ranch home has a small living room, dining room, and kitchen.

The raised ranch is a ranch house standing tall.

The tri-level home is a smug compromise.

Ah, suburbia! How diverse thou art -- the ranch, the raised ranch, the two story, and the tri-level.

The two-level house looks down condescendingly at its shorter neighbors.

The ranch home has one bathroom and, of course, an attached garage.

The top level of the two-story house is reserved for BRs and bath

You've come a long way from the simple log home -- or have you?

The lower level of the "tri" is for play.

The upper level of the raised ranch is simply the ranch raised.

The upper level of the "tri" is for the BRs and bath.

[Adapted from: Ron R. Allen and Ray E. McKerrow, The Pragmatics of Public Communication. (3rd Ed.), Dubuque, IA: Kendall-Hunt, 1985, pp. 101-102.]

CHAPTER 10.   USING LANGUAGE TO COMMUNICATE

CHAPTER CONTENT

Using Language Orally
Using Language Competently
    Effective Word Choice
    Definitions
    Imagery
    Metaphors
Using Language Ethically
    Ad Hominem Attack
    Linguistic Erasure
    Critiquing Domination
Selecting an Appropriate Style
    Serious Versus Humorous Atmosphere
    Ethical Moments: Doublespeak
    Speaker-, Audience-, or Content-Centered Emphases
    Propositional Versus Narrative Style
Selecting Language That Communicates Civility
    Gendered Versus Gender-Neutral Language
    How to Avoid Offensive Language
    The Problem of Uncivil and Hateful Speech
    The Commitment to Multicultural Visions of Audiences
Assessing a Sample Speech: "Coloring Outside the Lines: The Limits of Civility" by
    Raymie McKerrow
Chapter Summary
Key Terms
Assessment Activities
References

Discussion Questions

1. What are the multiple levels from which language gains meaning?
2   What does it mean to say that both language and language use are symbolic processes?
3. What is meant by these terms: encoding? decoding? denotative? connotative?
4. What is oral style?

5.   What are the characteristics of language in oral communication?
6.   What does it mean to say that speech is enthymematic?
7.   What are the essential features of effective word choice?
8.   Why is it important to use accurate language?
9.   How can a speaker use simplicity in language?
10.   What is the purpose of using signposts in a speech? transitions?
11.   What are preliminary summaries? final summaries?
12.   What kinds of relationships can be expressed through connectives or transitions?
13.   How can you communicate attitude through your choice of words?
14.   Provide a useful rule of thumb for language intensity.
15   Provide an example of each of the following kinds of definition: dictionary, stipulative, negative, etymological, exemplar, contextual, and analogical.
16.   What is imagery?
17.   How can a speaker use language to stimulate listeners' senses?
18.   What are the kinds of imagery available to the speaker?
19.   How can metaphors be useful to the speaker?
20.   What is meant by an ad hominem attack?
21.   What is the impact of linguistic erasure?
22.   What is meant by critiquing domination?
23.   What are some differences between serious and humorous style? When is each appropriate?
24.   What does it mean to be speaker-centered? audience-centered? content-centered?
25.   What are some differences between propositional and narrative style? When is each appropriate?
25.   Why is it important to consider the impact of gendered vs. gender-neutral langauge?
26.   What is especially problematic about uncivil or hateful speech?
27.   What is the role of a multicultural vision and why should we have one?

Questions to Stimulate Critical Thinking

1.   Do you think the essential features of effective speaking style can increase listener comprehension and retention? Why or why not?
2.   What kind of style do you have as a speaker? Describe it and assess the reactions of your listeners to it.
3.   Rhetorical critic Kenneth Burke suggests that words help shape our perceptions of people, events, social contexts, and the world. Do you think he is right? Why or why not?
4.   What metaphors are prevalent in contemporary socio-political discourse? Why do you think these metaphors have become dominant? What do they reveal or cover up?
5.   Can you make an argument of occasional imprecision in language? Provide some examples to support your position.

6.   Some psychologists argue that since words are the vehicles of thought, as our vocabulary increases, so does our ability to think and, ultimately, our intelligence. What are the implications of this theory for human communication?

7.   With the explosion of electronic media and information processing, some social observers are arguing that our society is becoming increasingly an oral society. The written style has given way to the oral. Do you think they're right? Why or why not? Defend your answer.

8.   What is the impact of linguistic erasure on community building?

9.   What does it mean to critique domination?

10.   What are some ways in which hate speech might be minimized?

11.   What are some ways to communicate a multicultural vision?

Application Exercises

1. Metaphor Make-overs

A. Objective: To facilitate students' ability to understand and employ metaphors.

B. Procedure: Use brainstorming to create a list of commonly used metaphors or provide them with such a list (for example, "busy as a bee," "slow as molasses in January," etc.). Re-write each worn metaphor. You may use the list at the end of this chapter to develop this exercise.

C. Discussion: When are common metaphors useful to a speaker? When should they be enlivened through new comparisons?

2. Opening "Doorways to the Mind"

A. Objective: To enhance appreciation of the potential of imagery in communicating ideas.

B. Procedure: Divide students into seven small groups and assign each group a type of imagery. Provide a general situation such as a bonfire at the beach, a rainstorm in a forest, etc. and ask each group to communicate something about the situation through the imagery they've been assigned. You may use the list provided at the end of this chapter for this exercise.

C. Discussion: What kinds of possibilities are opened up through the use of imagery? What potential is there for audience involvement in such images?

3. The Language of History

A. Objective: To increase understanding of language as a vital expression of contemporary thought.

B. Procedure: Provide students with copies of speeches from different historical periods or play several recorded speeches for students. You should choose speeches that are not familiar to students. After discussing the language usage in the speeches, you may want to ask students to rewrite several paragraphs for a contemporary audience. Compare with the original paragraphs.

C. Discussion: What was the time period of the speech? Who comprised the intended audience? What was the occasion? How could you determine these elements of the speech situation? How did the language of that time period differ from today's language?

4. Multiple Meanings

A. Objective: To underscore the fact that a single word can often have multiple meanings depending upon the listener.

B. Procedure: List several words on the chalkboard and ask students to write their meanings on a sheet of paper. Compare the answers. Your list might include:

cracked	book	spirit	black	high
lid	hot	down	fly	nickel

C. Discussion: Are the meanings of these words subject to variation? Why? How do meanings of words change? What factors affect them?

5. Language Intensity Chart

A. Objective: To alert students to the potential interaction of language choices and audience reaction.

B. Procedure: List approximately 20-30 words denoting objects, occupations, descriptors, or conditions on the chalkboard. Your list might include: dog, chair, nurse, judge, funny, red, ill, and so on. Ask small groups of students to make a chart of positive and negative words to substitute for those you have listed on the chalkboard. Compare lists.

C. Discussion: What are your reactions to the words which replaced the original list? How do you think an audience would react? When would a speaker choose such language? Follow up by discussing analogies. You may use the work sheet provided at the end of this chapter to guide your discussion.

6. Rhetorical Choices

A. Objective: To apply the understanding of language to specific examples of public speaking and to foster an appreciation for the function of language in speaking.

B. Procedure: Provide copies of one or more speeches for each student in class. You might use familiar speeches such as John F. Kennedy's inaugural or Martin Luther King's "I Have a Dream" speech or less familiar but equally interesting speeches such as Robert G. Ingersoll's eulogy for his brother, William Faulkner's acceptance of the Nobel Prize, or Alan Alda's graduation address, "From a Reel Doctor to Real Doctors." Ask each student to read the speech and note especially effective uses of language.

C. Discussion: What language uses did you note? Why? What other language choices could the speaker have made? Would they have been as effective? Why or why not?

How does the language create in the listener a new idea or a new way of seeing an old idea?

7. Additional exercises: Distribute and complete the Thinking about Language and Analogies forms at the end of this chapter.

Impromptu Speaking Exercises

1. Generic to Specific
   A. Objective: To increase the students versatility in concretizing general terms and adapting to their listeners.
   B. Procedure: Following a discussion of the usefulness of general and specific language to a speaker, ask each student to draw a prepared 3x5 card. Each card should have a single general term printed on it such as "freedom," "liberty," "generosity," "courage," etc. Ask each student to make the general term more concrete for the class in an impromptu speech using one or more of the language strategies suggested in the chapter.

2. Metaphors for Communication
   A. Objective: To stimulate creative thinking and develop alternative metaphors for the communication process.
   B. Procedure: Give each student several minutes to think of an appropriate metaphor or analogy for the communication process. You might provide an example to stimulate thought such as communication is like a football game or a flute-player or a tomato plant or a square dance. Ask each student to explain the analogy or metaphor they have chosen.

3. Predicting the Future
   A. Purpose: To enhance students' powers of description.
   B. Procedure: Ask each student to imagine where they will be, what they will look like, and what they be doing in 60 years. Each student should describe how and where they see themselves.

Additional Resources

Gschwend, Laura. "Acquiring the Artful Use of Antithesis." Speech Communication Teacher 9 (1995): 2-3.

Rowley, Edwin. "More Than Mere Words." Speech Communication Teacher 7 (1992): 5.

Rubin, Rebecca and Sally A. Henzl. "Cognitive Complexity, Communication Competence, and Verbal Ability." Communication Quarterly 32 (1984): 263-270.

Siddens, Paul. "Figures of Speech in Poetic and Everyday Discourse." Speech Communication Teacher 8 (1994): 13-14.

DEVELOPING IMAGERY

Think about each one of the scenes provided. Describe it in a short paragraph or series of statements that creates a vivid image for your reader or audience.

a high school basketball game
prom night
sunset at a beach
a walk through a woods on a moonlit night
sunrise on the North Pole
a roller coaster ride (like the Space Mountain)
a meal of cotton candy and licorice
the livestock exhibits at a county fair
a professional hockey game
a hospital ward
the local shopping mall
an elementary school lunchroom
a blue light special at KMart
a McDonald's restaurant
an open-air auction
a storm on the ocean
a snowfall in the city
a field of corn during a summer rain shower
a used car lot
the midway at the state fair
a bazaar in a foreign city
your library during final exam week
your parent's house
the vegetable aisle at your local supermarket
an art museum
Octoberfest in a small town
a beehive near a field of clover
a musical concert
an antique collector's exhibit
a Fourth of July parade
a horse show
a Christmas tree
an airport terminal
a crowded movie theater

THINKING ABOUT LANGUAGE

Mark each of the following propositions about the functions and value of language either true or false. You will probably want to discuss your answers with your classmates.

___ 1.   Language is what makes people human.
___ 2.   Each person has a unique style of speaking and writing.
___ 3.   Words can persuade people and, thus, have power.
___ 4.   Writing and speaking are both processes of discovery.
___ 5.   Language ability depends to some extent on the audience you are addressing.
___ 6.   We speak a different language from one audience to another, determined in large part, by the particular audience.
___ 7.   Language is so imprecise and unclear that you can never be certain another person really knows what you mean.
___ 8.   Verbal language is the most important aspect of communication.
___ 9.   Writing is a way of "concretizing" thought--of ordering nebulous ideas into concrete manifestations and meanings.
___ 10.   Nothing worth proving can ever be proven.
___ 11.   People should speak or write only when they feel they have something important to say.
___ 12.   People who say, "I just can't describe it" are really demonstrating the poverty of their linguistic ability.
___ 13.   The meaning of a word is an identifiable object or behavior in the empirical world.
___ 14.   Any discussion about language which uses language is pointless.
___ 15.   Writing and speaking frequently promotes fluency and adeptness in language usage.
___ 16.   A person's values and needs strongly influence their perceptions which, in turn, limit their ability to experience the world.
___ 17.   Experience precedes a sense of what is true which, in turn, comes before a sense of value.
___ 18.   The closer your language is to the mathematical in its precision, the clearer it is.
___ 19.   "It is sometimes possible to express an idea more precisely in bad English than in correct English." --St. Augustine
___ 20.   "You can indicate anything you see." --John Lennon
___ 21.   Words have different meanings to different people.
___ 22.   The English language is sexist.
___ 23.   Language reflects not only the personality of the user, but also the culture of their society.
___ 24.   Language creates our social reality.
___ 25.   To be useful and efficient, language must categorize and omit unique detail.

ANALOGIES: NEW IDEAS LINKED TO OLD EXPERIENCES

Often language stimulates our involvement when it is new and fresh. Thinking about ideas in new ways can be stimulated when we use analogies that juxtapose ideas and images. Consider the following examples:

1.   A head-on automobile crash at 40 miles-per-hour without a seatbelt would be like jumping from a third story building head-first into a cement sidewalk below.

2.   All of the McDonald's milk shakes sold to date would fill the gas tanks of every car in America.

3.   If all the Coca Cola sold were poured over Niagara Falls, the Falls would continue to flow at their normal rate for 16 hours and 48 minutes.

4.   If the 200 billion Oreo cookies sold since 1911 were stacked, they would reach to the moon and back 4 times.

5.   A three-year-old dog has reached the equivalent of 21 years in human age.

Now, think of analogies that will make the following images more vivid:

1.   What experiences are similar to the first few days on a major university campus?

2.   How anxious is a sixteen-year-old on a first date?

3.   What is it like to drift into sleep?

4.   How hard is it to decipher a page of calculus equations?

5.   What feelings do you have drinking ice water on a hot day?

REVITALIZING CLICHES

Substitute a more vivid word or phrase for each of the trite expressions listed below:

1. fit as a fiddle
2. as the crow flies
3. sharp as a tack
4. busy as a bee
5. white as a sheet
6. cool as a cucumber
7. dry as dust
8. too cute for words
9. a crying shame
10. down to earth
11. clear as mud
12. over and done with
13. at the crack of dawn
14. few and far between
15. between a rock and a hard place
16. stick to your guns
17. the picture of health
18. hungry as a bear
19. so hungry I could eat a horse
20. cold as ice
21. 'til hell freezes over
22. dark as night
23. hard as nails
24. quiet as a mouse
25. too funny for words
26. the good old days
27. so quiet you could hear a pin drop
28. follow in his footsteps
29. hot as Hades
30. stubborn as a mule.

CHAPTER 11.   USING VISUAL AIDS

CHAPTER CONTENT

The Functions of Visual Aids
Types of Visual Aids
      Physical Objects
      Representations of Objects and Relationships
      Representing Textual Materials
      Ethical Moments: Can Pictures Lie?
Acquiring Visual Aids
      How to Make the Most of Color Selection for Slides and other Visuals
      Making Your Own
      Downloading Visual Aids from the Web
      Getting Visual Aids from Research/Others
Strategies for Selecting and Using Visual Aids
      How to Select the Right Visual Aids
      Consider the Audience and Occasion
      Consider the Communicative Potential of Various Visual Aids
      How to Use Visual Aids Effectively
      Evaluate Computer-Generated Visual Materials
Chapter Summary
Key Terms
Assessment Activities
References

Discussion Questions

1. What is meant when we call it an "ocularcentric age?"
2. How might visual aids enhance speaker ethos?
4. What is the relationship between visual materials and persuasion of listeners?
5. What two large categories of visual aids can speakers draw from?
6. What kinds of animate objects might be considered for use as visual materials in a speech?
7. In preparing to use an animate object in a speech, what should the speaker consider?
8. What should be the main concern for a speaker who decides to use an inanimate object for visual material in a speech?

9.   What options are open for a speaker who cannot use an animate or inanimate object to visually reinforce a speech?

10.   What hints would you give a speaker who decided to use photographs as visual material in a speech? slides? videotapes? models?

11.   Give several situations for the use of chalkboard drawings or overhead projectors as visual aids.

12.   What types of graphs might a speaker use?

13.   What relationships are best represented by bar graphs? line graphs? pie graphs? pictographs?

14.   How does a speaker know which kind of graph to use? What are the advantages and disadvantages of each?

15.   What are flipcharts? flowcharts?

16.   What advice would you give a speaker who plans to give a handout to each member of the audience?

17.   How would you download visuals from the Web?

18.   What forms of visual materials encourage listener feelings in a speech? Which encourage listener thinking?

19.   What should you consider if you decide to use computer-generated visual materials in a speech?

20.   What impact does color have in enhancing PowerPoint slides?

Questions to Stimulate Critical Thinking

1.   Do you think the United States is the most visually oriented society in the world? Why or why not? What impact does this have on the way we communicate?

2.   In an ocularcentric society, do visual learners have an advantage over auditory and kinesthetic learners? What kind of learner are you?

3.   Why do you think visual aids affect listener comprehension and memory? The persuasive impact of messages?

4.   Can visual materials occasionally replace supporting materials? Why or why not?

5.   Which is probably more important in communicating your ideas to an audience--the words or symbols written on a speaker's poster or the way the speaker handles the poster?

6.   To what extent does the importance of visual material explain the popularity of television and film and the relative neglect of printed media in out society? Are there other factors to consider? What are they and how much impact do you think they have on our preference for the visual?

7.   Explain how the favors of attention might be considered when choosing or using visual materials in a speech.

8.   Research on color suggests that colors such as red, blue, silver, purple, and others can stimulate emotional responses in human beings. Speculate about the nature of those

responses.   Why do you think they occur?   Is it ethical to manipulate people by controlling the colors in their environment?

9.   When might a speaker decide it would be better not to use a visual aid in a speech? Provide the criteria for making such a decision. Defend your answers.

10.   Some research indicates that visualizing an experience can enhance performance. For example, if one visualizes making basketball free throws, accuracy actually improves. What effect do you think visualization would have for the public speaker anticipating an upcoming speech? Speculate on why visualization might be a successful technique for public speakers.

11.   Visual aids are increasingly becoming part of courtroom persuasion. Should they be banned from use in courtrooms to limit their potential influence?

Application Exercises

1. Considering the Options

A. Objective: To compel students to think beyond the obvious choices for kinds of visual material for speeches.

B. Procedure: Duplicate the Creating Visual Aids work sheet at the end of this chapter for your students. Divide students into groups or work with the class as a whole. Ask them to provide suggestions about the kinds of visual materials possible for each speech topic listed on the work sheet. Encourage creativity.

C. Discussion: What are the strengths and weaknesses of each kind of visual material? Do visual materials differ according to speech purpose?

2. Evaluating Visual Aids

A. Objective: To stimulate thinking about actual visual aids in everyday situations.

B. Procedure: Provide students with an opportunity to hear a live speaker who uses visual aids such as a member of the university forensics team, a Vacuum Cleaner salesperson, or a local insurance agency representative.

C. Discussion: Evaluate the use of visual aids. Consider the impact of the presentation without visual aids or if different kinds of visual aids had been used. You may use the visual aids critique form at the end of this chapter to guide the evaluation.

3. Visualizing Abstractions

A. Objective: To increase students' awareness of the power of visual aids to clarify abstract concepts.

B. Procedure: Generate a list of 10 to 20 abstract concepts and write them on the chalkboard.   Your list might include concepts such as "love," "charity," "eternity," "hedonism," and others. Then, consider visual aids that might clarify each of the abstract concepts.

C. Discussion: How effective are your visual aids in clarifying the abstract concepts? Are there any drawbacks in using visual aids to clarify abstractions? Can you think of examples where speakers used visual aids to clarify abstract ideas? When might you use visual aids to explain or clarify an abstract idea in a classroom speech?

4. Visual Aids in Your Classroom Speeches
    A. Objective: To provide feedback on the use of visual aids prior to the presentation of a classroom speech.
    B. Procedure: After making a speech assignment requiring the use of visual aids, pair students. Ask each pair to discuss the visual aids they have planned for the speech assignment. If possible, they should listen to the speech and observe the use of visual aids. Evaluate and make recommendations concerning the use of visual aids in the speech.
    C. Discussion: Did the visual aids add to the impact of the speech? Were they clear, well-prepared, easily seen, and generally effective? Did the visual aids capture listener attention? Was the presentation of the visual aids smooth? Were the visual aids relevant and appropriate? Were they adequately explained?

5. Using the Web and PowerPoint
    A. Objective: To increase expertise in the use of the Web and power point [requires a suitably equipped classroom].
    B. Procedure: Require the use of the Web or a PowerPoint presentation (1-3 slides) in a "one point speech" -- the objective is not to grade the speech content, but to evaluate the use and appropriateness of Web-derived and PowerPoint visuals.
    C. Discussion: Have the students evaluate each presentation as to its utility and appropriateness. Suggest other ways to use the Web or PowerPoint.

6. Additional exercise: Use the form for creating visual aids included at the end of this chapter. Share students' answers.

Impromptu Speaking Activities

1. Grab Bag Impromptu
    A. Objective: To give the student speaker an opportunity to practice using a visual aid.
    B. Procedure: Provide a grocery sack filled with items to demonstrate such as a can opener, a necktie, a cork screw, a calculator, etc. Ask each student to reach into the bag and choose an object, then demonstrate its use to the class in a short impromptu speech.

2. Chalkboard Impromptu

    A. Objective: To encourage students to practice controlling gestures and eye contact while using a visual aid.

    B. Procedure: Supply plenty of chalk and 4x6 cards. Either provide instructions on the 4x6 cards such as draw a tree or show us how to subtract 46 from 123 or ask students to write instructions on a card and exchange cards. Speakers should then follow the instructions on their cards, using the chalkboard to demonstrate. Stress audience involvement through eye contact and appropriate use of gestures and bodily stance during this impromptu.

Additional Resources

Danielson, M. "A Critical Thinking Approach to the Use of Visual Aids." Speech Communication Teacher 10 (1996): 8-9.

Diresta, Diane. Knockout Presentations : How to Deliver Your Message With Power, Punch, and Pizzazz. Worcester, MA: Chandler House Press, 1998.

Downing, Joe and Cecile Garmon, "Teaching Students in the Basic Course How to Use Presentation Software," Communication Education 50 (2001): 218-29

Gutgold, Nichola D. "Pointing Groups to PowerPoint," Speech Communication Teacher 13 (1999): 5

Hibben, J. "A Key Address." Speech Communication Teacher 10 (1996): 9-10.

Raines, Claire, Linda Williamson and Tony Hicks, Using Visual AIDS : A Guide for Effective Presentations. Menlo Park, CA: Crisp Publications, 1995.

Robbins, Jo. High-Impact Presentations : A Multimedia Approach. New York: Wiley, 1997.

Weadock, Glenn E. and Emily Sherrill Weadock. Creating Cool Powerpoint 97 Presentations. Foster City, CA: IDG Books Worldwide, 1997.

GUIDELINES FOR AUDIO-VISUAL AIDS USE

Ask yourself the following questions as you prepare your audio-visual aid:

1. Is it large enough to be seen by everyone without straining?
2. Is all printing or other marking short and simple?
3. Is the aid colorful and involving?
4. Can I use it without blocking the audience's view of the aid and will I remember to always keep my eyes on my listeners?
5. Will a pointer be helpful?
6. Will I hold the aid steady and long enough to give my audience enough time to look at it carefully?
7. Can I avoid distraction by keeping the aid covered or out of sight before and after it is used?
8. Can I fit the aid into the speech as more than simply an ornament?
9. Can I avoid making the aid the most important aspect of the speech?
10. Have I practiced enough with the aid before the speech so that using it will be natural, comfortable, and flow smoothly in the speech?
11. Have I made all the necessary arrangements for use of special equipment?
12. Since handing materials out is distracting to me, my listeners, and the next speaker, can I avoid doing this?
13. Will I have all my materials close a hand during the speech? Walking around to retrieve aids provides disorganization cues for my audience.
14. Have I planned how I will lay aside or cover the aid after using it?
15. Do I know how much time showing the aid will take? It's counted in the total speech time.
16. Do I know exactly when I'll use the aid so its timing is accurate?
17. If I'll need assistance, have I planned for it in advance?
18. Can I avoid reaching across my body (for example, to point to a chart) or waving the aid in front of my face?
19. If I have a chart or poster, will it be secured in some fashion so I don't have to hunt for it on the floor in the middle of my speech?
20. Am I ready to set up my visual aid so I don't keep my audience waiting?

VISUAL AID ASSESSMENT FORM

Name:

Speech Topic: <u>Comments</u>

Quality
      increases understanding
      scholarly value
      completeness of information
      adds to the development of ideas

Preparation
      attention gaining
      colorful/involving
      neatness
      large enough to be seen easily
      secured to prevent falling

Presentation
      integrated well into speech
      adequate explanation
      nondistracting
      covered before and after use
      timing
      gestures--avoid reaching across body
                use of pointer
                materials close at hand

Main Strength:

Main Weakness:

Total points awarded _____
Total points possible _____

CREATING VISUAL AIDS

Several speech topics are listed for informative and persuasive speeches. Record as many suggestions as you can for visual aids that could be used to enhance a speech on each topic.

Informative Speech Topics:

1. A visit to Europe
2. Weather prediction
3. Palmistry
4. Cooking with a wok
5. Coins of the world
6. Migration patterns of hummingbirds
7. Breeds of cats
8. World Cup Soccer
9. Contact lenses
10. Carbon molecules

Persuasive Speech Topics:

1. Donate your blood (or organs)
2. Vote Republican or Democratic
3. Begin an exercise program (or diet)
4. Take an extra/elective science course next term
5. Give money to a local charity
6. Fasten your seatbelt
7. Be a designated driver
8. Invest $10.00 a week in the mutual funds
9. Travel on your own overseas

CHAPTER 12.   USING YOUR VOICE AND BODY TO COMMUNICATE

CHAPTER CONTENT

Orality and Human Communication
        Aggregative
        Agonistic/Invitational
        Ethically Appropriate
Public Speaking as a Social Performance
Using Your Voice to Communicate
        How to Determine Your Delivery Time
        Perceptions of the Speaking Voice
        Controlling the Emotional Quality
        Practicing Vocal Control
        How to Improve Your Voice
Using Your Body to Communicate
        Assessing Different Dimensions of Nonverbal Communication
        Adapting Nonverbal Behavior to Your Presentations
Chapter Summary
Key Terms
Assessment Activities
References

Discussion Questions

1.   How would you distinguish between and among Ong's characteristics of orality?
2.   What is meant by an "invitational rhetoric?"
2.   What is meant by "kairos?"
3.   What is the function of synchronicity?
4.   What four factors constitute vocal intelligibility?
5.   What should you consider in adjusting your loudness level as you speak?
6.   What is considered a normal rate of speech? What factors affect speech rate?
7.   What is enunciation?
8.   What is the difference between pronunciation and dialect?
9.   What are vocal stereotypes? How do they affect speaker credibility?
10.   Why is it important to vary rate, pitch, stress, and pauses?
11.   What is pitch? optimum pitch level? pitch variation? How do they affect vocal quality?

12.   How can a speaker use vocal stress to enhance a message?
13.   Explain the differences between helpful and distracting vocal pauses.
14.   What are emotional characterizers? How are they important to the speaker?
15.   What is the best way to master vocal control?
16.   What three generalizations about nonverbal communication should guide your speechmaking?
17.   What is proxemics? What are its components?
18.   How can proxemics help a speaker create a particular physical and psychological impact on an audience?
19.   How do movement and stance function as nonverbal cues in public speaking?
20.   How do facial expressions function to control communication?
21.   What are affect displays?
23.   What are the three kinds of gestures commonly used by speakers?
24.   What factors influence the effectiveness of gestures?
25.   What nonverbal channels speakers have to consider in creating effective messages?

Questions to Stimulate Critical Thinking

1.   When might it be unethical to allow the power of the voice to carry an idea?
2.   When might an "invitational rhetoric" be called for?
3.   The word "stereotype" generally carries a negative connotation. Is it always negative? Can you think of exceptions?
4.   What vocal stereotypes do we assign to certain voices--for example, women with very low pitched voices, men with high voices, or adolescents whose voices occasionally crack. What image do you think your voice projects?
5.   Assuming you have a personal preference for maintaining certain distances from others in interpersonal, group, and formal settings, where do you think these preferences originated? How do you know if they are shared by others? What role does culture play in these preferences? Provide several intercultural examples if you can.
6.   Does the gender of the speaker impose certain social stereotypes on acceptable nonverbal behavior in the delivery of a speech? If so, which behaviors are affected and how?
7.   A widely-quoted study by Albert Mehrabian concludes that nonverbal elements of messages account for an overwhelming percentage of what a receiver perceives. Do you think nonverbal communication is more important than the content of a speaker's message?
8.   Can effective delivery compensate for an otherwise ineffective or weak speech? Defend your position on this issue.
9.   What can a speaker do to raise the emotional involvement of an audience during a speech? Is it ethical to stimulate an emotional reaction in an audience? Why or why not?

10. Select a public speaker you feel is especially effective and analyze his or her nonverbal behavior. Using the criteria established in your textbook, explain why this person is effective.

11. To what extent is nonverbal communication determined by cultural norms?

Application Exercises

1. Countdown
   A. Objective: To improve flexibility in vocal delivery.
   B. Procedure: Assign students roles such as a parent scolding a child or emotions such as love or hatred they are to display for the rest of the class using numbers instead of words. The class may participate by guessing what emotion or situation is being played.
   C. Discussion: Determine how effectively students are able to convey thoughts without using traditional language. Identify certain cultural norms which are available for conveying feelings.

2. Poetic License
   A. Objective: To improve a student's ability to use the components of vocal delivery to enhance the meaning of a message.
   B. Procedure: Provide copies of a poem for students or ask that they bring their favorite to class. Students should read the poem to the rest of the class in a manner that adds to the meaning they see in the poem.
   C. Discussion: What components of vocal delivery discussed in the text are students able to identify? What components offer the most difficulty for students?

3. Vocal Identification
   A. Objective: To discover the nature of our vocal stereotypes.
   B. Procedure: Prior to class, record the voices of several friends. Playback the recordings and ask students to jot down the answers to a number of questions such as: What is the person's gender, age, height, weight, socio-economic status, employment, personality characteristics, etc.? Compare answers, then provide a correct answer to each question.
   C. Discussion: How accurate were the student answers? What accounts for the differences in answers (e.g., could students correctly determine the person's gender, age, height, weight, etc. from the voice alone)? What kinds of emotions were you able to identify in the vocal recordings? How well do you think an individual's personality is conveyed vocally?

4. Experimenting with Proxemics
   A. Objective: To test the relationship of physical distances and emotional responses.

B. Procedure: Pair students and ask each pair to stand at a distance they feel comfortable while maintaining eye contact; then have one student begin to walk toward the other --at what point does the 'other' begin to back up? Ask students to approximate the distance at which they felt uncomfortable.

C. Discussion: Do the distances at which students feel uncomfortable vary? Why or why not? Did eye contact seem to have an impact on physical proximity? Why or why not? What effect might cultural differences have (in the event there are not persons from varied cultures in class) on distance? How can knowledge of proxemics be used in speaking to audiences?

5. Gestures that communicate

A. Objective: To illustrate the power of gestures in conveying meaning.

B. Procedure: Working in groups of 3-4, use gestures in such a way that others in the small group can identify the meanings that follow:

      1. Absolutely not
      2. Give it to me (or ... to her/him)
      3. You're out of your mind
      4. Whatever
      5. What are we going to do?
      6. I've done all that I can do - what else do you expect?
      7. She scored! The World Cup is ours!!
      8. Let me think about that

C. Discussion: Which gestures appear to be culture specific -- are there different gestures that would communicate the same idea in another culture? How would you find out?

[Adapted from Ronald R. Allen and Raymie E. McKerrow, The Pragmatics of Public Communication. 3rd ed., Dubuque, IA: Kendall-Hunt, 1985, p. 186]

6. Field Study

A. Objective: To increase students' awareness of the variety and function of nonverbal communication around them.

B. Procedure: Pair students and send them to specific locations such as a street corner, elevator, library, grocery store (you may need a manager's permission for this), busy doorway, etc. Ask students to take notes unobtrusively about the behavior they observe. When they return to class, students should share their observations of nonverbal behavior with the class.

C. Discussion: What kinds of nonverbal behaviors occurred? Did patterns of behavior or rules seem to emerge? How did nonverbal and verbal behavior interact? Did nonverbal behavior encourage, discourage, or replace verbal behavior? Did you notice anything unusual in nonverbal behaviors?

7. Watching the Soaps

    A. Objective: To investigate the impact of nonverbal communication.

    B. Procedure: Bring a videotape segment of a television drama or soap opera to class. Play the videotape with the sound turned off. Ask the class to speculate about the dialogue. Rewind and play the segment with the sound turned on.

    C. Discussion: How accurate were the speculations about the dialogue? How did viewers reach conclusions about the dialogue without actually hearing it? What do characters reveal with their dress, gestures, facial expressions, and eye contact? Which nonverbal messages seemed most important? Were different interpretations of these messages possible?

8. Additional Exercises: Practice articulation and movement with the two exercises included at the 'end of this chapter.

Impromptu Speaking Activities

1. "The One That Got Away"

    A. Objective: To provide students with practice in the dimensions of nonverbal communication.

    B. Procedure: Ask students to draw predetermined topics such as describe the fish that got away, tell us what it would be like to be caught in the eye of a tornado or show us how to start up a motor.   Each topic should require that the student use physical or vocal delivery to enhance listeners understanding of the topic.

2. Using Your Voice

    A. Objective: To focus students' awareness on the potential for adding meaning to messages through vocal variety.

    B. Procedure: Provide students with short passages that require some vocal interpretation to enhance meaning. For the sake of interest, the passages should not be the same. Ask each student to deliver the message facing away from the class or standing behind a screen. Meaning should primarily be enhanced through vocal delivery.

3. Role Playing

    A. Objective: To project and identify nonverbal behaviors that add understanding to verbal communication.

    B. Procedure: Ask several pairs of students to prepare and then present a short dialogue and the accompanying nonverbal messages for a variety of situations. You might include the following:

        ---two people who meet on the street and talk but neither is sure who the other is

---a student who needs to take a make-up exam trying to get a classmate to give him or her the answers

---a visitor trying not to insult a friend whose obnoxious pet keeps trying to climb into his or her lap

---a server trying to get a larger tip from a customer

---a friend visiting a hospital patient who tries not to reveal that the patient is terminal

---a purchaser of illegal merchandise meeting a contact, neither is certain that the other is the right person

---a homeowner trying to politely refuse the merchandise of a door-to-door salesperson

---a flight attendant trying to get a passenger to cooperate by fastening a seat belt

Additional Resources

Avdeyeva, Tatyana V. "Practicing Delivery Skills,"Speech Communication Teacher 13 (1999): 9-10

Hayward, Pamela. "Delivery Cards." Speech Communication Teacher 8 (1994): 3.

Sonandré, Debbie Ayres and Joe Ayres, "Practice Makes Perfect," Speech Communication Teacher 13 (1999):14-15.

ARTICULATION EXERCISE

Find a partner in class and take turns reading these tongue-twisters aloud, slowly at first, gradually increasing speech with each reading. Afterwards discuss the value of clear, crisp articulation in public speaking and make suggestions for improving articulation.

1.   Six slim sleek saplings.

2.   Stop at the shop at the top of Schram Street.

3.   In January and February there are few athletic exhibitions.

4.   Some shun sunshine; some shun shade.

5.   He whittled a white whistle from the willow wand which he cut.

6.   Shoes and socks shock my shy sister Susan.

7.   Fill the sieve with thistles, then shift the thistles through the sieve.

8.   The freshly fried flesh of flying fish is fine dining.

9.   Much whirling water makes the mill wheel work well.

10.   She sells sea shells, does he sell sea shells too?

VOCAL DELIVERY ASSESSMENT FORM

Name of Speaker _____

Rate the speaker on each of the vocal elements of delivery listed. Also provide comments and reasons for your ratings.

5 = excellent 4 = good 3 = average 2 = fair 1 = poor

VOCAL ELEMENT   RATING   COMMENTS
_____

Rate

_____

Volume

_____

Pitch

_____

Inflection

_____

Articulation

_____

Pronunciation

_____

Vocal Quality

_____

Conversationality

PHYSICAL DELIVERY ASSESSMENT FORM

Name of Speaker _____

Rate the speaker on each of the physical elements of delivery listed. Also provide comments and reasons for your ratings.

5 = excellent 4 = good 3 = average 2 = fair 1 = poor

PHYSICAL ELEMENT   RATING   COMMENTS

Posture

_____

Confidence

_____

Appearance

_____

Facial Expression

_____

Eye Contact

_____

Movement

_____

Gestures

_____

Use of Notes

CHAPTER 13.   SPEECHES TO INFORM

CHAPTER CONTENT

Facts, Knowledge, and the Information Age
Motivational Appeals: Engaging Listeners Where They Are
    Classifying Motives
    Motive Clusters
    Using Motivational Appeals in Speech Preparation
    Ethical Moments: Your Ethical Boundaries
Essential Features of Informative Speeches
    Clarity
    How to Use Psychological Principles for Clarity
    Associating New Ideas With Familiar Ones
    Relevant Visualizations
Types of Informative Speeches
    Definitional Speeches
    Instructional and Demonstration Speeches
    Oral Briefings
    Explanatory Speeches
Assessing a Sample Speech: "The Geisha" by Joyce Chapman
Chapter Summary
Key Terms
Assessment Activities
References

Discussion Questions

1.   Distinguish between facts, information, and knowledge.
2.   Explain the differences between behavior that results from biological needs and social motives.
3.   What are the categories in Maslow's Hierarchy of Needs?
4.   What does the phrase "hierarchy of prepotency" mean and how do the five levels of Maslow's hierarchy of needs function as a prepotent hierarchy?
5.   According to McClelland, what three primary clusters identify motive types?
6.   What kinds of motives would be found within each cluster? Give examples of motives that might be used to appeal to audiences from within each cluster.

7. How does a motivational appeal function with respect to "verbal depiction" and "verbal association?"
8. How can a speaker decide which motive appeals to use in a speech? for an audience?
9. What can you do to achieve clarity in an informative speech?
10. How can a speaker associate new ideas with familiar ones?
11. Why should we cluster ideas in three to five headings in a speech?
12. What are relevant visualizations in a speech? How can a speaker create them?
13. What is the goal of an effective definitional speech and how does effective structuring assist in meeting that goal?
14. Distinguish between instructional and demonstration speeches.
15. What should the introduction for a demonstration speech accomplish?
16. What determines if a briefing is general or technical?
17. What guidelines govern an effective briefing?
18. What is the purpose of an explanatory speech?
19. What are the biggest challenges in developing a speech of explanation?
20. Provide some guidelines for structuring an explanatory speech.

Questions to Stimulate Critical Thinking

1. Do "facts" exist objectively or is all information subject to human interpretation via communication? Debate the issue and defend your position with examples or other evidence.
2. Do you think all human motives are instinctual or do you think some can be learned? Give examples to support your opinion.
3. Do you think animals and humans share similarities in motivations? If so, what are they? If not, why not?
4. How can a speaker determine which of the motive clusters identified by McClelland will work with potential audience members?
5. Which of the motive clusters appeals most to you? Why? Identify people for whom the other motive clusters might hold more appeal.
6. Some research suggests that visualization plays an integral role in maximizing physical performance such as in shooting free throws or executing difficult dives. How do you think visualization influences behavior?
7. Several scholars argue that a "choice of words is really a choice of worlds." Do you agree? Why or why not?
8. Can you identify motive clusters other than those included in your textbook? How can these motive clusters be used?
9. What ethical boundaries should govern the use of motivational appeals?
10. Are motivational appeals more crucial in persuading listeners than logical appeals? Defend your position.

11.   Discuss the problem of information retention and the forgetting curve. What techniques seem to enhance memory? Why? Can you think of applications of these techniques in your own life?

12.   Occasionally, in spite of exactly the same information, people come to diametrically opposed conclusions. How can this phenomenon be explained?

13.   Do you think an individual's particular world-view or cultural background influences his or her interpretation of information? How?

14.   Can information ever be presented in a neutral fashion? Some scholars claim that nothing is ever neutral. Reject or defend their position.

Application Exercises

1. Identifying Basic Appeals
   A. Objective: To gain expertise in identifying appeals that are commonly used.
   B. Procedure: Bring to class a videotape containing recent television ads -- ask students to identify the various appeals used in each of the ads. Replay the ads 2-3 times and have students work in small groups to discuss and label the various appeals used.
   C. Discussion: Using the 'motive clusters' and Maslow's hierarchy -- discuss how the various appeals identified -- how effective are they? What other appeals might work better?

2. Applying Maslow's Hierarchy of Needs
   A. Objective: To understand how Maslow's Hierarchy of Needs varies from person to person.
   B. Procedure: Identify three or four hypothetical audience members whose demographic characteristics vary significantly. List the hierarchy of needs on the chalkboard. For each hypothetical audience member, describe what might be included in each level of the hierarchy.
   C. Discussion: How do physical and safety needs vary among people? What can satisfy belongingness and love needs for individuals? How can esteem and self-actualization needs be met for different people? How can the recognition of varied needs among people help the public speaker?

3. Designing a Political Campaign
   A. Objective: To adapt motive clusters to audiences.
   B. Procedure: List several different audiences on the chalkboard. Assign student teams and ask each team to choose a political candidate (contemporary or historical) to represent in a campaign. Using the motive clusters, teams should develop a campaign message adapted to two of the audiences listed on the chalkboard.

C. Discussion: Which motive clusters are most often used for each audience? Why? How do messages incorporate motive clusters? Can messages be adapted to include several motive clusters at one time? How can students in a public speaking classroom use motive clusters in their messages to classmates?

4. Defining Concepts

A. Objective: To allow students to practice associating new ideas with familiar ones.

B. Procedure: Divide students into small groups and ask each group to associate a new concept (either assigned or developed by the group) with familiar ones using the different methods of definition developed in the text.

C. Discussion: Are some methods of association more effective than others in creating understanding? What is the most practical method for implementation of this strategy for the speaker?

5. Strategies for Informative Speaking

A. Objective: To offer students an opportunity to recognize the strategies and choices available to the informative speaker.

B. Procedure: Provide the students with an example informative speech. You may use one of the speeches included in the text, a speech printed in an anthology or Vital Speeches of the Day. After reading the speech, analyze the choices the speaker made and identify the strategies for presenting information to an audience.

C. Discussion: How do variables such as audience and occasion influence the speaker's choice of information? Do these variables affect the manner in which the speaker presents information? How can a speaker reinforce information for listeners without boring or offending them? What role do transitions and other organizational cues play in transmitting information effectively? Can you think of ways that this speech might have been improved?

6. Evaluating Informative Speaking

A. Objective: To apply the principles of informative speaking in the evaluation of a sample informative speech.

B. Procedure: Provide a videotaped informative speech and ask students to evaluate it using the guidelines for effective informative speaking. They might evaluate one of their own videotaped informative speeches.

C. Discussion: What are the requirements for effective informative speaking? How closely did the speech you saw conform to those requirements? How would you suggest that the speaker improve the speech?

7. Teaching Excellence
    A. Objective: To analyze speeches of explanation in the classroom.
    B. Procedure: Ask students to think of the most effective lecture they experienced in the past several weeks or months. Briefly describe the content of the lecture.
    C. Discussion: What made the lecture memorable? What principles of effective explanations did the instructor employ? How can you use the same principles in your speeches of explanation?

8. Demonstrations
    A. Objective: To plan the organization for a speech of demonstration
    B. Procedure: Brainstorm for topics for speeches of demonstration. Record the topics on the chalkboard. Divide students into small groups and give each group several demonstration speech topics. Ask them to develop an organizational pattern for each topic. Share the results with the class.
    C. Discussion: Which patterns of organization were used most frequently to organize these speeches? Which patterns of organization work best with demonstration speeches? Why? What problems does a speaker face when planning a speech of demonstration? Suggest some solutions to those problems.

9. Motivational Appeals -- Additional Applications: At this point, you may wish to include a discussion of the speaker's responsibilities in choosing motivational appeals. Complete the exercises on Developing Audience Appeals and American Motives included at the end of this chapter.

10. Informative Speeches -- Additional Applications: Use the Impromptu Quotations Assignment included at the end of this chapter. You may also require an oral briefing and use the outline and assessment forms at the end of this chapter to develop this assignment.

Impromptu Speaking Activities

1. The Speaker's Options
    A. Objective: To encourage students to use a range of motivational appeals in their speaking.
    B. Procedure: Have students bring their textbooks to class; using the list of motives within each cluster, assign a student to each specific motive (some may have more than one student assigned). Select a general topic that would be suitable for a potential speech in class. Ask each student to construct a motivational appeal for the speech using the motive they've been assigned. Each student should then explain the kind of appeal and how it would work on the speech topic in an impromptu manner.

2. Famous Quotations
    A. Objective: To develop the qualities of effective informative speaking.
    B. Procedure: Photocopy and distribute the list of famous quotations which follows this chapter. At random, give a student a specific quotation and give her or him 30 seconds to prepare. After preparation time, each student given a quotation then speaks for 2 minutes giving a brief explanation of what the quote means (in their view - what is the importance of the quote?). Students should observe the qualities of effective informative speaking as they explain their quotations.

3. Hometown Highlights
    A. Objective: To provide an opportunity for students to provide information to others from their personal experience.
    B. Procedure: Ask students to think about a special feature of their hometown. Then, each student should share information about that hometown highlight with the class in an impromptu speech.

Additional Resources

Fowles, Jib. "Advertising's Fifteen Basic Appeals." <u>American Mass Media: Industries and Issues</u>. Ed. Robert Atwan, et al. New York: Random House, 1986, pp. 43-54.
Rowan, Katherine. "New Pedagogy for Explanatory Public Speaking: Why Arrangement Should Not Substitute for Invention." <u>Communication Education</u> 44 (1995): 236-250.
Rowan, Katherine. "The Speech to Explain Difficult Ideas." <u>Speech Communication Teacher</u> 4 (1990): 2-3
Yamasaki, Joan. "Teaching the Recognition and Development of Appeals." <u>Speech Communication Teacher</u> 8 (1994): 12-13.

DEVELOPING AUDIENCE APPEALS

Propose the best motive appeals for the following speech topics and audiences. Note: would everyone in the audience be against the topic? How might you use audience analysis techniques to discover whether your 'stereotype' of the audience's presumed negative stance on your topic is accurate?

1.   Topic: Affirmative action should be eliminated.
        Audience: Members of the Black Students Association.

2.   Topic: Monogamy is the best form of marital relationship.
        Audience: Mormons practicing polygamy.

3.   Topic: Pacifism is the only morally defensible approach to international conflict.
        Audience: Subscribers to Combat Arms magazine.

4.   Topic: Gun control legislation should be passed.
        Audience: Members of the National Rifle Assn.

5.   Topic: The University of Tennessee women's basketball team is the best in Divisoin One.
        Audience: The University of Connecticut's women's basketball booster group.

6.   Topic: Capital punishment is inhumane.
        Audience: A woman whose husband and daughter were gunned down in front of her.

7.   Topic: Living together is better than marriage.
        Audience: Fundamentalist religious couples celebrating their 50th wedding anniversaries.

8.   Topic: Violent protest is the only way to bring about fundamental social change.
        Audience: A Quaker meeting.

9.   Topic: Rap music is an important form of social expression.
        Audience: A group of Baptist ministers.

10.   Topic: Most American business persons lack ethical standards.
        Audience: National Assn. of Marketing and Management.

AMERICAN MOTIVES

Commonly cited proverbs often tell us a great deal about the thinking of the people who state them. Consider the following proverbs often quoted in our society. What do they tell you about our values, beliefs, and attitudes?

1. A penny saved is a penny earned.
2. Beauty is as beauty does.
3. Look before you leap.
4. You can't fight city hall.
5. Still waters run deep.
6. Spare the rod and spoil the child.
7. Don't switch horses in midstream.
8. People who live in glass houses shouldn't throw stones.
9. A rolling stone gathers no moss.
10. Where there's smoke there's fire.
11. A bird in the hand is worth two in the bush.
12. You can't judge a book by its cover.
13. Better late than never.
14. You can't teach an old dog new tricks.
15. Don't count your chickens before they're hatched.
16. When the cat's away, the mice will play.
17. Don't cry over spilled milk.
18. Don't spit into the wind.
19. A stitch in time saves nine.
20. Beauty is only skin deep.
21. A watched pot never boils.
22. All that glitters is not gold.
23. You can lead a horse to water, but you can't make him drink.
24. He who hesitates is lost.
25. Haste makes waste.
26. He who laughs last, laughs best.
27. Time heals all wounds.
28. Like father, like son.

ORAL BRIEFING OUTLINE

Name:
Topic:
General Purpose:

Specific Purpose:

Pattern of Organization:

I.   Introduction
      A.   Type of introduction:

      B.   Attention-gaining strategy:

      C.   Preview of main ideas:

      D.   Transition to body of speech:

II.   Body of speech
Attach a list of your main ideas and subordinate ideas in appropriate outline form and indicate each of the following on your outline:
      A.   Internal summaries

      B.   Transitions and signposts

      C.   Organizational pattern for subpoints in each area

III.   Conclusion
      A.   Type of conclusion

      B.   Transition from body of speech to conclusion:

      C.   Summary of main ideas:

      D.   Closing statement:

IV.   Bibliography: (list author, title, publishing data and pages cited)

ORAL BRIEFING ASSESSMENT FORM

Name:

Topic:	Comments
Introduction	
attention	
preview	
credibility	
Organization	
clear progression	
adequate explanation	
transitions	
within time limits	
Visual Aid	
quality	
timing	
presentation	
integration	
effectiveness	
Physical and Vocal Delivery	
conversational style	
vocal volume	
eye contact	
poise & confidence	
gestures	
desire to communicate	
Conclusion	
adequate summary	
development	
interest	

Main Strength:

Main Weakness:

Total points awarded ____   Total points possible ____

FAMOUS QUOTATIONS IMPROMPTU

Directions: Ask each student to choose and develop one quotation by applying it to something in their lives, providing an example to amplify the idea, or explaining the meaning of the quotation. The criteria for developing an effective explanation should be used to explain and evaluate the assignment.

1. "Better one bird in the hand than ten in the wood." John Heywood, Dialogue on Wit and Folly

2. "Up, sluggard, and waste not life; in the grave will be sleeping enough." Benjamin Franklin, Poor Richard's Almanac

3. "Laziness travels so slowly that poverty soon overtakes him." Benjamin Franklin, Way to Wealth

4. "Life is like a fire; it begins in smoke, and ends in ashes." Old Arab proverb

5. "Children and fools cannot lie." John Heywood, Proverbs

6. "Remember that time is money." Benjamin Franklin, Advice to a Young Tradesman

7. "Life is one long process of getting tired." Samuel Butler, Note-Books

8. "Indeed, a friend is never known till a man have need." John Heywood, Proverbs

9. "Money is a good servant, but a bad master." H.G. Bohn, Handbook of Proverbs

10. "Nothing but money is sweeter than honey." Benjamin Franklin, Poor Richard's Almanac

11. "Money is the best bait to fish for man with." Thomas Fuller, Gnomologia

12. "It is better to live one day as a lion than a hundred years as a sheep." motto on an Italian 20-lire silver piece about 1930

13. "It is not how long, but how well we live." John Ray, English Proverbs

14. "A little neglect may breed mischief; for want of a nail the shoe was lost, for want of a shoe the horse was lost, and for want of a horse the rider was lost." Benjamin Franklin, Poor Richard's Almanac

15. "The Lord prefers common-looking people. That is the reason He makes so many of them." Abraham Lincoln

16. "It is better to know some of the questions than all of the answers." James Thurber

17. "A man may well bring a horse to the water, but he cannot make him drink without he will." John Heywood, <u>Proverbs</u>

18. "Praise makes good men better and bad men worse." Thomas Fuller, <u>Gnomologia</u>

19. "A man is rich in proportion to the number of things which he can afford to let alone." Henry D. Thoreau, <u>Walden</u>

20. "There never was a good war or a bad peace." Benjamin Franklin, letter to Josiah Quincy

21. "No man ought to look a gift horse in the mouth." credited to Jerome in the 300's

22. "Time heals what reason cannot." Seneca, <u>De Ire</u>

23. "And when he is out of sight, quickly also is he out of mind." Thomas a Kempis, <u>Imitation of Christ</u>

24. "Women's faults are many,
      Men have only two;
      Everything they say,
      And everything they do."   source unknown

25. "After the event even a fool is wise." Homer, <u>Iliad</u>

26. "That bird is not honest that fouleth his own nest." John Skelton, <u>Poems against Garnesche</u>

27. "When poverty comes in at the door, love leaps out at the window." Thomas Fuller, <u>Gnomologia</u>

28. "There can no great smoke arise, but what there must be some fire." John Lyly, <u>Euphues</u>

29. "Knowledge is power." Thomas Hobbes, <u>Leviathan</u>

30. "Words are the dress of thoughts; which should no more be presented in rags, tatters, and dirt, than your person should." Lord Chesterfield, <u>Letters</u>

CHAPTER 14.   SPEECHES TO PERSUADE AND ACTUATE

CHAPTER CONTENT

Contemporary Approaches to Changing Minds and Behaviors
    VALS: Adapting Messages to Listeners' Psychological Orientations
    How to Use VALS to Craft a Persuasive Message for a Diverse Audience
    Communication Research Dateline: Resistance to Counterpersuasion
    PRIZM: Adapting Messages to Listeners' Behavioral Patterns
    Reference Groups: Adapting Messages to Listeners' Group Loyalties
    Credibility: Adapting Messages to Your Own Strengths
Basic Types of Persuasive and Actuative Speeches
    Persuasion as Psychological Reorientation
    Persuasion as Impetus to Action
Structuring Persuasive and Actuative Speeches
    Ethical Moments: Using Fear Appeals
    Using the Motivated Sequence for Psychological Reorientation
    Using the Motivated Sequence for Behavioral Actuation
Assessing Sample Speeches: "Speech for Impeachment" by Rep. J. C. Watts and
"Speech Against Impeachment" by Rep. Richard Gephardt
Chapter Summary
Key Terms
Assessment Activities
References

Discussion Questions

1.   What does persuasive speaking attempt to accomplish?
2.   Compare informative to persuasive speaking. What are the similarities? differences?
3.   What is the nature of "good reasons?"
4.   What does the phrase "psychological orientation" refer to?
5.   What does VALS stand for? What does it identify? How would you use VALS as a speaker?
6.   What initial attitudes toward your speech topic and purpose might an audience display?

7.   What suggestions would you give a speaker to help design a speech taking into account the audience's predispositions toward the topic?

8.   When should a two-sided speech be used?

9.   What is saliency? How does it affect the speaker's choices?

10.   What is PRIZM and how does it differ from VALS?

11.   What are reference groups and how do they affect the development of persuasive and actuative speeches?

12.   How does credibility affect successful persuasion?

13.   How do speeches of reinforcement and modification function to reorient listeners?

14.   How does one use the motivated sequence in speeches aimed at psychological reorientation?

15.   How does one use the motivated sequence in speeches aimed at behavioral actuation?

Questions to Stimulate Critical Thinking

1.   Describe the ways you can resist counterpersuasion. How well do you think you resist counterpersuasion?

2.   How can you adjust your speech messages to take maximum advantage of reference group information?

3.   Suggest some ways you can enhance your personal credibility during the persuasive process.

4.   Explain the psychological basis for the approach to changing beliefs developed in your textbook. What assumptions about human beings are made in this approach? Do you agree? Why or why not?

5.   Are some people naturally more easily persuaded than others? If so, what distinguishes these people? Why are they more easily persuaded? How easily persuaded do you think you are?

6.   Under what conditions would a persuasive effort be deemed unethical? What should any persuader be held accountable for in asking for your approval?

7.   Does self-persuasion exist? If so, what is it? How does it work? What role does it play in other forms of persuasion?

Application Exercises

1. Applied Persuasion

   A. Objective: To identify the kinds of persuasive ends that may be used.

   B. Procedure: Ask students to note as many examples of speaking to reinforce, promote psychological change, or actuate that have occurred in their interactions with others in the past week or so - and to bring the list of occurrences to the next class period. Compare the responses in isolating the kinds of ends that are sought.

C. Discussion: What distinguishes the forms of speaking? What characterizes each form? Can various persuasive purposes be combined?

3. Evaluating Persuasion

A. Objective: To evaluate persuasive speaking in various forms.

B. Procedure: Refer students to an example speech in the textbook or play a videotaped speech such as the one available from your textbook representative. Analyze and evaluate the persuasion. You may wish to use the evaluation sheets at the end of this chapter.

C. Discussion: What strategies does the speaker use to persuade? How effective do you think they are?

4. Understanding Psychological Orientation (VALS)

A. Objective: To apply the Values and Lifestyles Program.

B. Procedure: Divide the chalkboard into nine columns and label each column for one of the nine lifestyles: survivors, sustainers, belongers, emulators, achievers, "I-am-mes," experientials, socially conscious, and integrated people. Discuss the characteristics of each group and then list groups of people that you think fit the characteristics.

C. Discussion: How does each group reflect a constellation of attitudes, beliefs, opinions, hopes, fears, and so on? What does this system of categorizing people assume about their behavior and thinking? Do you agree or disagree? Which group fits you most closely? How would a speaker use this system in planning a speech to persuade?

5. Adapting PRIZM to Speech Preparation

A. Objective: To use PRIZM in gaining a better understanding of the audience that you will be attempting to persuade.

B. Procedure: Use the following "clusters" as described in the text – have small groups of students select a topic, and analyze how the topic would be developed to appeal to each "cluster":

Towns and Gowns
Starter Families
Boomtown Singles
Middleburg Managers
Upward Bound

C. Discussion: Have each group report its conclusions and ask others to critique the approach of the group. What are the possible weaknesses of this approach?

6. Recognizing Salient Authorities
   A. Objective: To stimulate reflection about citing authorities.
   B. Procedure: Divide students into small groups. Give each group ten minutes to decide on a hypothetical speech topic and five credible authorities to cite in the speech. Share the conclusions.
   C. Discussion: What determines the credibility of an authority? What determines the saliency of authorities? How can a speaker determine which authorities will be most effective with an audience?

7. Additional Exercises: If time permits, this is an appropriate place to begin introducing students to the concept of speech criticism, in particular, that criticism functions partially as persuasion/argument.

Impromptu Speaking Activities

1. Problem-Solution Impromptu
   A. Objective: To provide students with an experience in using motivational appeals in specific scenarios.
   B. Procedure: Use the prepared scenarios provided at the end of this chapter. Ask each student to choose one, then present a persuasive solution to the problem.

2. Applying the Motivated Sequence
   A. Objective: To provide experience in applying the motivated sequence to persuasive speeches.
   B. Procedure: Ask each student to think of an appropriate persuasive topic, then describe in an impromptu speech what would be contained in each step of the motivated sequence on that topic.

3. Group Persuasion
   A. Objective: To actively involve audience members in the persuasion process while allowing speakers to adapt and react in their persuasive efforts.
   B. Procedure: Separate and move the classroom chairs to two sides of the classroom; label one side "pro" and the other "con" (or "for" and "against"). Ask an individual or a small group of students to persuade audience members on an assigned topic. Allow audience members to shift their seating from one side of the room to the other if their opinions are changed during the course of the speech. The number of seat changes

should be recorded as an indicator of persuasion. Note: If your classroom is large enough, chairs can be separated into 5 groups--strongly for, for, neutral, against, strongly against. Voting takes place in the same manner as before as students shift their seats to indicate persuasive effects of the speech.

4. Analyzing Advertisements
    A. Objective: To integrate textbook theory with real world persuasion.
    B. Procedure: Either bring a video in with current ads, or ask if a few students with VCR's could bring some into the class; use the videos to discuss what works and what doesn't in persuading consumers.

Additional Resources

Cammilleri, Sandra. "Creating Persuasive Commercials." Speech Communication Teacher 9 (1995): 10-11.

Cialdini, Robert B. Influence: The Psychology of Persuasion. Rev. Ed. Quill, 1993.

Garrett, Roger. "The Premises of Persuasion." Speech Communication Teacher 5 (1991): 13.

Gass, Robert H. and John S. Seiter. Persuasion, Social Influence, and Compliance Gaining. New York: Prentice Hall, 1998.

Hodak, James M. and Julia A. Skeen, "Commercial Persuasiveness: A Tool for Active Audience Analysis." Speech Communication Teacher 12 (Summer 1999): 14.

Petty, Richard E. and John T. Cacioppo, Attitudes and Persuasion: Classic and Contemporary Approaches. Boulder, CO: Westview Press, 1996.

PROBLEM-SOLUTION IMPROMPTU

Consider the following scenarios and provide a persuasive solution in a short impromptu.

1.   You are an intelligent, "A" student. You take the Graduate Record Examination test and do very poorly. As a result, you do not get into the graduate school of your choice. Discuss the problems of aptitude or intelligence testing and provide some reasonable solutions for a better graduate admissions standard.

2.   You are a student majoring in political science. Just before you turn in a major assignment for class, you discover that your roommate who is also in the class has copied your assignment and turned it in ahead of you. Discuss the problem of cheating in academia and propose some solutions.

3.   After several months of blissful marriage you begin to find ticket stubs and love notes in your spouse's pockets. Then your spouse forgets to come home several nights a week. You realize there's a problem. Discuss infidelity and the rising divorce rates.

4.   Your roommate has developed strange habits of late. You find your roommate chewing breath mints by the roll, undergoing strange changes in mood, and even occasionally reeling down the halls of your dorm. Then you discover a bottle of vodka under your roommate's bed. Consider the problem of alcohol abuse and potential cures.

5.   You've just had your tonsils removed. Upon changing doctors, you learn that you really didn't need the surgery after all. Your doctor informs you that many people are being "taken" on unnecessary surgeries. Inform us about the problem of unnecessary surgeries and provide some solutions for coping with this problem.

6.   As you raise a glass of tap water to your lips, you notice the grey-green color of the water and suspended particles floating in it. You've recently read about your city's difficulties in finding sources of plentiful, clean water. Discuss the diminishing supply of uncontaminated water in the United States.

7.   You spend an evening in your favorite lounge with friends, some of whom smoke. Although you don't notice at the time, the air around you is blue with cigarette smoke. The next morning your eyes burn, you cough, and your hair and clothing reeks of cigarette odor. Discuss the problems of the non-smoker in this society.

8.   You read an ad in the back pages of a sleazy magazine and decide to order the product. After weeks of anxious anticipation you realize you've been the victim of mail order fraud. Discuss the problem and provide a solution.

9.   One of the largest purchases of your entire life is your dream home. You settle in and enjoy the prestige of owning your own property. The first few weeks go smoothly, then you notice that the roof leaks when it rains. Several days later, the kitchen sink quits working and then the garage door falls off. Discuss the increasingly poor quality of American workmanship.

10.   You are an executive secretary with an important, well-paying position in a large firm. You boss has recently been making physical passes at you in the office. Today your boss, despite a marriage of 25 years, 4 children, and 6 grandkids, has invited you out for a candlelight dinner at a romantic hideaway. You hesitate because you know you couldn't find another job like the one you now have. Discuss the problem of sexual harassment on the job and provide a solution for it.

11.   You have just put your kids to bed. After turning off their light, you realize that they are "glowing in the dark." Appalled, you recall that the children had X-rays taken at the doctors office today. Suddenly you realize that there may be a problem with too many X-rays. Discuss the problem of X-rays and provide a solution which states how one could cut down on the number of X-rays taken.

12.   Late one evening you observe your neighbor sneaking around his house with a gasoline can. Hours later the house burns to the ground and within months your neighbor is awarded a hefty insurance settlement. Discuss the fastest growing crime in American---arson.

13.   You are doing some early holiday shopping. Walking down the aisle of a local department store, a man brushes up against you. It is not until you go to purchase an item that you notice your wallet has been stolen. Discuss the problem of pick-pockets and propose some solutions which might help a shopper.

14.   You live in Love Canal, New York. You've notice an increase in birth defects over the past few years. You've notices that your house is sinking into the ground. You've also noticed that the members of your family are more sick than usual. Then you discover that you are living on top of a chemical waste dump. Outraged, you voice your feelings. Discuss why there is a problem with chemical waste dumps and provide a solution for the problem.

15.   You park your 2-month-old Porsche to do some shopping in Cincinnati and return several hours later to find only a grease spot. You've been ripped off. Discuss the problem of chop shops and provide a solution for them.

16.   For the last three weeks you've had an uncontrollable urge to beat up your mother-in-law who lives with you. You tie her to a chair and steal her social security check. You are a parent abuser. Discuss the problem regarding children who abuse their elderly parents. How might this problem be solved?

17.   You are 15 years old and you have decided to marry your 13-year-old stead. You get your parent's permission. With a blood test and a $5.00 marriage license, you'll enter the institution of matrimony. Discuss the problems of teenage marriage and provide possible solutions.

18.   You figure the boss won't notice so you slip a few pencils from work into your pocket to take home. A large corporation won't even notice the loss. A few days later, you take a pad of paper and a stapler. Discuss the rising rate of white collar pilfering on the job and present some solutions.

19.   On a college course field trip to the state penitentiary, you are appalled at the crowded conditions, noise, and violence. Five prisoners are confined to cells built for two, the walls echo with taunts and jeers, and three inmates suffered stab wounds last week. Discuss some of the problems associated with prison overcrowding and suggest some viable solutions.

20.   As you're driving home one afternoon, you notice that a vehicle pulls out in front of you from its parking spot near a local tavern. The driver weaves down the road and swerves in and out of the oncoming lane of traffic. Convince us that drunk driving is a serious problem and give us some solutions which might help solve the problem.

21.   A recent news report tells of three Nazis and a religious fanatic who hijack an atomic energy plant threatening to blow up the world if their demands are not met. Fortunately, the gang is captured and locked away. However, the problem of nuclear blackmail is increasing. Discuss it and provide some solutions.

22.   A friend asks you to help plan the funeral of a relative. You agree and both of you consult the local funeral director. He tells you the arrangements have been made and takes care of every detail. The funeral is handled efficiently and sympathetically. Two weeks later you receive a bill for $12,000. Discuss the rising cost of dying in America and provide some solutions.

23.   Your neighbor's dog has been harassing your cat. You notice that the dog has been gone for several days only to find her back in your yard again but this time with 12 puppies. The

future for kitty looks grim. Discuss the exploding pet population problem in the U.S. and propose some controls.

ATTITUDE REINFORCEMENT ASSESSMENT FORM

Speaker _____ Topic _____
Specific Speech Purpose:

Audience Pre-Speech Attitude:

Expected Audience Post-Speech Attitude:

Subject	1 2 3 4 5 6 7 8 9 10
original	
clear & specific	
related well to audience	
Introduction	1 2 3 4 5 6 7 8 9 10
gained attention	
provided reason to listen	
clear preview of ideas	
Organization	1 2 3 4 5 6 7 8 9 10
clear pattern of development	
effective transitions	
overall unity	
adequate development	
Conclusion	1 2 3 4 5 6 7 8 9 10
summarized main theme	
effective audience appeal	
motivating/inspiring	
Motive Appeals	1 2 3 4 5 6 7 8 9 10
relevant to audience	
consistent throughout speech	
adequate intensity	
adequate variety	
Supporting Material	1 2 3 4 5 6 7 8 9 10
adequate quantity	
appropriate for audience	
reinforcing	
related to audience needs	
Tone/Atmosphere	1 2 3 4 5 6 7 8 9 10
appropriate for occasion	
adapted to topic & speaker	
reinforced through language choices	
reinforced through speaker enthusiasm	
Delivery	1 2 3 4 5 6 7 8 9 10
vocal style adapted to topic	
effective use of vocal emphasis	
adequate vocal volume & rate	
reinforcing gestures	
adequate eye contact	
confident and enthusiastic	

Overall Evaluation of Effectiveness:

PERSUASIVE SPEECH ASSESSMENT FORM

Student Name: _____ Student Topic: _____

Speech Structure and Organization		Speech Delivery	
Attention Statement	0 1 2 3	Eye Contact	0 1 2 3
Reason to Listen	0 1 2 3	Voice Volume	0 1 2 3
Direction	0 1 2 3	Intensity	0 1 2 3
Transitions/Signposts	0 1 2 3	Posture	0 1 2 3
Supporting Materials	0 1 2 3	Movement	0 1 2 3
Logic & Reasoning	0 1 2 3	Composure	0 1 2 3
Summary/Reiteration	0 1 2 3	Use of Notes	0 1 2 3
Motivational Appeal	0 1 2 3	Adaptation	0 1 2 3
Ethical Appeal	0 1 2 3	Visual Support	0 1 2 3
Persuasive Strategy	0 1 2 3	Distractions	0 1 2 3

General Comments:

Sub-Total Points: _____   Time Limit Penalty: _____

Speech Length: _____   TOTAL SCORE: _____

CHAPTER 15.   ARGUMENT AND CRITICAL THINKING

CHAPTER CONTENT

Argument and Cultural Commitments
    Commitment to Change Your Mind
    Commitment to Knowledge
    Commitment to Worthy Subjects
    Commitment to Rules
Argument as Justifying Belief and Action
    Types of Claims
    Evidence
    Forms of Reasoning (Inference)
    Ethical Moments: The Use of Evidence
    Testing the Adequacy of Forms of Reasoning
    Detecting Fallacies in Reasoning
    How to Test Arguments
A Model for Organizing and Evaluating Arguments
How to Develop Argumentative Speeches
Assessing a Sample Speech: "Mending the Body by Lending an Ear: The Healing Power of Listening," by Carol Koehler
Chapter Summary
Key Terms
Assessment Activities
References

Discussion Questions

1.   How is critical thinking related to your everyday life?
2.   Explain the connection between critical evaluation and argumentation.
3.   What are you committed to if you engage in public argument?
4.   What do we mean when we say that argument is more thoroughly rule-governed than other forms of public presentation?
5.   What is a claim?
6.   What does a claim of fact assert and what questions should be asked about it?

7.   What is a claim of value? policy?

8.   What four questions should you ask when establishing or analyzing a policy claim?

9.   What is rationally relevant evidence? What considerations help determine what is rationally relevant evidence?

10.   What is motivationally relevant evidence and how might it be selected?

11.   Provide an explanation or definition of reasoning.

12.   How does reasoning from examples or inductive reasoning connect evidence to a claim? reasoning from generalization or axiom? reasoning from sign? reasoning from parallel case? reasoning from causal relations?

13.   What are the primary tests for reasoning from example? reasoning from generalization/axiom? reasoning from sign? reasoning from parallel case? reasoning from causal relations?

14.   What is a fallacy in reasoning?

15.   What are the most common fallacies? Provide an example of each.

16.   Explain the six elements that make up argument according to Stephen Toulmin.

Questions to Stimulate Critical Thinking

1.   Is the judgment of whether reasoning is "logical" culturally based? If so, how? Can you provide an example of the logical structures accepted by another culture?

2.   How can a listener or speaker detect fallacies in reasoning?

3.   What practical suggestions can you offer for developing arguments?

4.   How should a speaker go about rebuilding an argument that another has attacked? How should a speaker prepare for this possibility?

5.   The textbook lists a number of fallacies. Can you think of additional ones? List and explain them.

6.   What do you do if an audience is not open to reasoning? In what other instances does the use of argumentation fail in our society?

Application Exercises

1. Chain Arguments

   A. Objective: To improve students' abilities in framing arguments and identifying forms of reasoning.

   B. Procedure: Provide an argument using one of the forms of reasoning described in the text. Designate a student who will then identify the form of reasoning in your argument and state another argument. The next student identifies the reasoning and launches another and so on.

C. Discussion: Are any of the arguments faulty? If so, why? What would strengthen the argument? Are some forms of reasoning more convincing than others? Why?

2. Hyde Park Forum

A. Objective: To encourage students to formulate messages that will withstand refutation.

B. Procedure: Select three controversial propositions for which there would be a variety of responses. Have each student develop a pro or con position on the propositions. On three consecutive days, hold "open hearings" on each of the propositions. Make sure there are enough students on each side of the issue to encourage lively debate.

C. Discussion: Analyze the strength of various arguments. What role did evidence play in them? logic?

3. The Presidential Debates

A. Objective: To introduce an element of real world advocacy as well as offer students an opportunity to identify arguments and evaluate their relative strengths.

B. Procedure: Obtain and play one or segments of several of the debates prior to a presidential election. Periodically, stop the tape and evaluate the arguments used by the participants.

C. Discussion: What are the claims being made? What kind of evidence and reasoning are used? Which arguments are strongest/weakest? Why? How could a weak argument be strengthened? Who "won" the debate? Why?

4. Detecting Fallacies

A. Objective: To increase the recognition of fallacious reasoning.

B. Procedure: Have students bring in editorials from recent campus or community newspapers that they have evaluated for the presence of fallacies. Have students work in groups to discuss the fallacies they have located in their respective editorials. Once finished, have groups report on the most common fallacies they have uncovered.

C. Discussion: Which fallacies did you detect? Explain why the reasoning is fallacious. Substitute a sound argument for the fallacious reasoning.

5. Claims of Fact, Value, and Policy

A. Objective: To help students understand the differences among claims of fact, value, and policy.

B. Procedure: Explain the three types of claims and provide several examples of each. Provide a claim and ask students to re-frame it. For example:

1. There is no speed limit on some highways in the western United States. (Claim of fact, re-frame as policy or value)

187

2. All parents should install a V-chip to screen out television violence. (Claim of policy, re-frame as fact or value)

3. Freedom of speech is fundamental for high-quality journalism. (Claim of value, re-phrase as fact or policy)

C. Discussion: What are the differences among claims of fact, value, and policy? Are some claims more common than others for persuasive speeches? What differences in development are required for claims of fact? value? policy?

6. Understanding Arguments

A. Objective: To understand, using the Toulmin model, the relationship between elements of argument.

B. Procedure: Individually or in small groups, ask students to isolate each element in a sample argument that you have provided (without identifying labels - see sample below). For example:

"The latest FBI statistics show that rape is up" (Evidence). Mandatory minimum penalties for rape should probably be instituted (Claim with Qualifier). Rape always increases when rapists think they will not pay for their crimes (Warrant). Rape is most often a crime of opportunity and rapists stalk their victims (Backing for Warrant). Unless the rape victim is also murdered (Reservation).

C. Discussion: Discuss the relationship between the Warrant and the Data, as well as why backing might be necessary in this instance. Discuss the relationship between the possibility of the reservation being true, and the status of the qualifier.

7. Additional Exercises: You may wish to use the forms included at the end of this chapter for Real World Arguments, Reasoning Patterns, Identification of Claims and Beliefs, Arguing Value Claims, and Informal Fallacies. Assessment forms for various speaking assignments are also included.

Impromptu Speaking Activities

1. Tag Team Debate

A. Objective: To provide experience in forming arguments and responding to attack.

B. Procedure: The class period before the debate, select a controversial topic with which students are familiar and divide the class into "pro" and "con" groups -- endeavor to have about equal size groups. Ask the students to simply think about the issue and come to class with one -two arguments in support of their side. At the next class, begin with a student from the Pro side, and have her/him present an argument. That student then "tags" a student on the "Con" side to refute the argument presented, and to present a new argument. The altering of sides continues until everyone has had a chance to speak.

2. Division of the House

A. Objective: To integrate the practice of advocacy and cross-examination skills.

B. Procedure: Decide on a topic with clear "pro-con" sides or dimensions. Ask all students who favor the topic to sit on one side, with those opposed on the other. Indicate that first students will speak on each side of the issue, and that then, others will be allowed time to cross-exam the speakers–each side taking turns Designate 2-3 students to offer arguments for the Pro side (2-3 minutes per student. Shift sides and repeat for the Con side. Once this is completed, ask if any students wish to shift to the other side, or to move to a middle "undecided" position. Then proceed to cross-examination–allowing any student from the Con side first to cross-exam speakers from the Pro side for 4-5 minutes, then switch sides to allow the Pro side to cross-exam Con speakers.

3. Small Group Debates

A. Objective: To provide additional experience in developing arguments.

B. Procedure: Select teams toward the end of one class period; have the students in each group select a controversial topic and decide who will be pro and who will be con. The task is for students to invent/research arguments in support of their side; you can also prescribe the kind of arguments to be created (as in an argument from cause and one from example). At the next class period, have each group come to the front of the class and, beginning with one person on Pro, then one on Con, have them begin an argument. Chaos may reign supreme in this assignment as students begin to argue out of turn, ask questions, etc. Use this as an opportunity to illustrate argument strengths, questioning techniques, etc. as events suggest.

Additional Resources

Bozik, Mary, "Fact or Opinion," Speech Communication Teacher 13 (1999): 14-15.

Hamlet, J. "Editorial Sessions: A Different Approach to Teaching Argumentation." Speech Communication Teacher 9 (1994): 8.

Hollihan, T. A. and K. T. Baaske, Arguments and Arguing: The Products and Processes of Human Decision Making. Prospect Heights, IL: Waveland Press, 1998.

Katsion, John R. "Mock Parliamentary Debate," Speech Communication Teacher 13 (Winter 1999): 12-14.

Makau, Josina M. and Debian L. Marty, <u>Cooperative Argumentation: A Model for Deliberative Community</u>. Prospect Heights, IL: Waveland Press, 2001.

Martin, Steven, "Stock Issues-Based Policy Speech Small Group Exercise." <u>Communication Teacher</u> 14 (2000):13-14.

Rieke, Richard and Malcom O. Sillars, <u>Argumentation and Critical Decision Making</u>. 5th ed., New York : Longman, 2001.

Shelton, M. "Analysis of Editorial Cartoons--An Alternative Approach to Teaching Argumentation." <u>Speech Communication Teacher</u> 10 (1995): 11-12.

Spicer, Karin-Leigh and William Hanks. "Critical Thinking Activities for Communication Textbooks." <u>Speech Communication Teacher</u> 7 (1993): 6-7.

Inch, Edward S. and Barabara Warnick, <u>Critical Thinking and Argumentation</u>. 4th ed., Boston: Allyn & Bacon, 2002.

REAL WORLD ARGUMENTS

We are often faced with situations in which we need to logically construct an argument. You may have to persuade others to see things your way. To successfully argue your point of view you need to use claims, reasoning, and supporting material. For each of the following claims, develop at least two forms of reasoning and supply several kinds of supporting material.

1.   I deserve a raise of $500 a month.

2.   Our company should develop a department of communication.

3.   Employees should not use the company phone (or fax machine) for personal business.

4.   This company should reimburse me for all expenses incurred during my business trips.

5.   Our company should develop a program for parental leave.

6.   Men are promoted more often than women in this company.

7.   We should have a day care center for working parents.

8.   Every employee should get his/her birthday off with pay.

9.   Retirement should not be mandatory at age 65.

10.   I deserve my own reserved parking space near a main entrance.

11.   We need a union to protect workers' rights and salaries.

12.   You should tie up your dog so that he doesn't dig up the petunias in my yard.

13.   You should put my automobile repair job at the top of your priority list.

14.   The accident was not my fault.

15.   I don't want to purchase your product.

16.   Your bank should give me the personal loan.

17.   I will not pay the invoice until your company satisfactorily completes the work.

REASONING PATTERNS

Identify the kind of reasoning in each of the following examples:

_____ 1.   Since I started taking vitamins I've had so much more energy.

_____ 2.   That man was present at the murder scene with the murder weapon in his hand. Looks like he's the murderer.

_____ 3.   Everyone knows that children from broken homes are the juvenile delinquents of tomorrow. I expect to see the neighbor kids in court some day. Ever since the divorce, their parents have had nothing but trouble with them.

_____ 4.   This spring has been just like the spring of '75. We can expect a hot, dry summer.

_____ 5.   Carol and Jim both got good grades in that class. I'm going to take it to boost up my grades.

_____ 6.   I've been on that diet for 3 weeks now and my social life has really improved. I should have dieted years ago.

_____ 7.   I think arthritis runs in the family. I hope I don't suffer from it like my sister has.

_____ 8.   Socialized medicine works so well in Great Britain, I think we should try it here.

_____ 9.   The last four cars we've had have been Fords and they've run so well, we're going to buy another one.

_____ 10.   Russia peasants who live into their 100's eat a diet of mainly yogurt. I'm eating more yogurt these days too.

_____ 11.   The airplane has disappeared from the radar screen and broken radio contact. It must be down.

_____ 12.   There are always light on at their house late into the night. They must have lots of parties.

_____ 13.   My cat ate that new cat food and got sick. I'm not buying it anymore.

_____ 14.   I don't believe she'll graduate in just 2 1/2 years. It's going to take me four.

_____ 15.   Isn't it obvious to you that our foreign aid policy is ludicrous? The U.S. has lost billions of dollars in Vietnam, Angola, and Iran.

_____ 16.   Let's run for cover! With all those dark clouds over there, it'll be raining in a minute.

_____ 17. I really liked "Bonanza" and "Gunsmoke," I think I'll tune in to that new western scheduled for Monday night.

_____ 18. Your skin is cold, clammy, and blotchy. I bet you're coming down with something.

IDENTIFICATION: CLAIMS & BELIEFS

Identify claims of fact, value, policy or beliefs, attitudes, and values among the following:

_____ 1.   Washington was a greater president than Lincoln.
_____ 2.   Student fees at my university are higher than any   other state school.
_____ 3.   Intercollegiate athletics builds character.
_____ 4.   President Lyndon Johnson was a high school debater and later a debate coach before he became president.
_____ 5.   President Johnson was a highly skilled debater.
_____ 6.   I think Clinton should have been impeached.
_____ 7.   Anyone who burglarizes is a scumbag.
_____ 8.   Parking tickets should be abolished.
_____ 9.   President Reagan was a brilliant TV star.
_____ 10. I'm especially fond of parties.
_____ 11. The earth is flat.
_____ 12. Most leprechauns have warts.
_____ 13. It's too stuffy in here. We should open a window.
_____ 14. Martha should shut up and go home.
_____ 15. Saturn makes the best car on the road.
_____ 16. I know Bruno.
_____ 17. My sister should have her nose fixed.
_____ 18. Blue is a peaceful color.
_____ 19. However, black is nice too.
_____ 20. I like orange best of all.
_____ 21. Prince Charles is tall, dark and homely.
_____ 22. Toadstools are delicious.
_____ 23. I hate Reeboks.
_____ 24. We should have more fortune hunters in today's world.
_____ 25. Drive safely and save lives.
_____ 26. Chewing gum causes cancer.
_____ 27. Loreal products should be boycotted - they use animals in research.
_____ 28. Rainwater contains dangerous bacteria.
_____ 29. I'm afraid to cross the Arrowhead Bridge in the dark.
_____ 30. My fairy godmother wears spectacles.
_____ 31. I should have gone home right after school.
_____ 32. Time will tell.
_____ 33. You can't teach a new dog old tricks.
_____ 34. Spiders are cute.

195

ARGUING VALUE CLAIMS

Determine the best arguments for each of the following value claims:

1. Coke is it!! (Not Pepsi)

2. Americans should eat more popcorn.

3. The three bears ought to press charges against Goldilocks for breaking & entering.

4. Pit Bulls are better than Beagles.

5. Lavender is a feminine color.

6. Ohio University is as good as Harvard.

7. Benjamin Franklin once argued that the wild turkey should be adopted as the national symbol of the U.S. He was right. We should dump the bald eagle.

8. Fish are freer animals than birds.

9. If the Hindu religion is right and we are destined to be reincarnated as another life form after we die, it would be better to come back as a spider than as a rattlesnake.

10. Women make better diplomats than men.

11. Men are more open-minded than women.

12. It would be better for someone stranded on an uninhabited island with no hope for rescue to have a subscription to Reader's Digest than The Wall Street Journal.

13. Cats are smarter than dogs.

14. It would be worse to be a compulsive gambler than a compulsive drinker.

15. Webster's Dictionary is the most useful book ever compiled.

16. McDonald's is a better place to eat than Taco Bell.

17. Fords are better than Chevies.

18. It is better to grow up in a city than on a farm.

19. It is best to be the middle child in a family of three.

20. We should abolish national secretary's week.

21. Wheaties is the best breakfast food available.

22. The Beatles contributed more to music than did Beethoven.

23. Throughout history cows have been more helpful to humans than horses.

INFORMAL FALLACIES

Given the text's discussion of fallacies, identify each of the following:

_____ 1.   I've had a stomachache all day, and I know why. Last night at dinner something told me I shouldn't eat those evil-looking mushrooms.

_____ 2.   Have you tried Babbles, the new effervescent breakfast food? Since Babbles is on more breakfast tables than any other cereal, there's no question about its quality.

_____ 3.   And listen to what Betty Crabapple, your favorite TV star, says about Babbles, "They're simply delish."

_____ 4.   If the prosecuting attorney doesn't stop his attack on my client, an innocent citizen, no one will be safe from this malicious persecution.

_____ 5.   The young groom, on his first shopping trip, went looking for some tomatoes. In a vegetable shop he saw a bushel basket full of them. After examining 2 or 3 on top and finding them satisfactory, he concluded that all of them were good, so he bought the whole basketful.

_____ 6.   Last month I read three nineteenth century novels, and they certainly were dull. After this, I'll stick to the twentieth century.

_____ 7.   No mathematician has ever been able to demonstrate the truth of the famous "lost theorem" of Fermat, so it must be false.

_____ 8.   Russian threats are no news. Therefore Russian threats are good news, since no news is good news.

_____ 9.   The army is notoriously inefficient, so we cannot expect Major Smith to do an efficient job.

_____ 10.   I am sure that their ambassador will be reasonable about the matter. After all, humans are rational animals.

_____ 11   Mr. Scrooge, my husband certainly deserves a raise in pay. I can hardly manage to feed the children on what you have been paying him.

_____ 12.   Governor Jones stands for freedom, integrity and efficiency in government.

_____ 13.   For sale: Chow dog, eats anything, very fond of children.

_____ 14.   Suckers and malcontents are always with us, always ready to support some visionary scheme to get something for nothing out of the state. That's why we should reject the Desmond bill.

_____ 15.   It is necessary to confine criminals and to lock up dangerous lunatics. That's why there is nothing wrong with depriving people of their liberties.

_____ 16.   Join the few, the proud, the Marines!

_____ 17.   Isn't it true that students who get all A's study hard? So, if you want me to study hard, professor, the best way to do it is to give me A's in this course.

_____ 18.   A foreman is fired by the XYZ canning company. He gives a newspaper interview charging unfair labor practices in the cannery. A cannery official declares, "The foreman is sore about being fired. He's a troublemaker and was once convicted of embezzlement."

_____ 19.   Fifty thousand women can't be wrong.

_____ 20.   Some thieves are arguing over division of seven pearls worth a king's ransom. One of them hands two to the man on his right, then two to the man on his left. "I," he says, "will keep three." The man on his right says, "How come you keep three? "Because I'm the leader." "Oh. But how come you're the leader? "Because I have more pearls."

_____ 21.   George Washington warned against entangling foreign alliances. Invited on all sides to internationalist adventures, we should remember the wisdom of the Father of our Country.

_____ 22.   My cold began to get better the day after I took Sniffleless. I recommend it.

_____ 23.   Peter is trying to persuade Paul to address the Dahlia Growers Association. "What do you mean you can't make a speech? You have a lot to say about the growing of dahlias, from the 12 foot tree variety to the Unwin dwarfs. Anybody who has something to communicate can tell his friends about it. Anybody can make a speech, Peter!"

_____ 24.   "Dad, you don't need to worry about lending me the money for this new business. I'll pay you back just as soon as profits start coming in."

_____ 25.   I guess it's safe to eat these; they look just like the mushrooms we have at home.

_____ 26.   Of course he's selfish--he's a man, isn't he?

_____ 27.   If God had meant women to have red toenails, He would have made them red in the first place.

_____ 28.   If we don't execute murderers, they'll take over the streets.

_____ 29.   There are three Gamma Delts in my physics class. Invariably they get the lowest scores on exams. Gamma Delts must not be very smart.

_____ 30.   Everybody agrees. Chicago is a great city!

_____ 31.   If we let gay couples adopt children, the AIDS epidemic will spread, people will be too sick to work, businesses will fail, and our democracy will collapse.

_____ 32.   Dave usually wins any argument with his girlfriend when he makes her too angry to talk by pointing out that her eyebrows grow together over the bridge of her nose.

REFUTATION SPEECH ASSESSMENT FORM

Name:

Topic:

CONSTRUCTIVE SPEECH   <u>Comments</u>

Organization

  adequate introductory preview

  clear pattern

  adequate explanation

  transitions & internal summaries

  adequate development of summary

  within time limits

Argument

  clear argument claims

  reinforcing supporting materials

  appropriate source citations

  adequate reasoning

Physical and Vocal Delivery

  enthused & animated

  eye contact

  confident & sincere

  vocal quality

REBUTTAL SPEECH   <u>Comments</u>

Organization

  clarity of development

  logical progression

  adequate introduction & conclusion

Analysis

  sufficient supporting material

  development of impact of arguments

  logical argument

  clear attack on opponent's position

Delivery

  enthused & animated

  eye contact

  confident & sincere

  vocal quality

Total points awarded ____

Total points possible ____

SHIFT OF OPINION SCALE

Place a number ranging from 1 (weak) through 7 (strong) in the most appropriate blank. The outside positions (1 and 7) indicate extremes; the central positions (especially 3, 4, 5) denote more moderate reactions.

Your name:

Speaker's name: Speaker's topic:

Your pre-speech attitude toward the topic:

        disagreed strongly ___ ___ ___ ___ ___ ___ ___ agreed strongly

Your post-speech attitude toward the topic:

        disagreed strongly ___ ___ ___ ___ ___ ___ ___ agreed strongly

---

Your name:

Speaker's name: Speaker's topic:

Your pre-speech attitude toward the topic:

        disagreed strongly ___ ___ ___ ___ ___ ___ ___ agreed strongly

Your post-speech attitude toward the topic:

        disagreed strongly ___ ___ ___ ___ ___ ___ ___ agreed strongly

---

Your name:

Speaker's name: Speaker's topic:

Your pre-speech attitude toward the topic:

        disagreed strongly ___ ___ ___ ___ ___ ___ ___ agreed strongly

Your post-speech attitude toward the topic:

        disagreed strongly ___ ___ ___ ___ ___ ___ ___ agreed strongly

CHAPTER 16. BUILDING SOCIAL COHESION IN A DIVERSE WORLD: SPEECHES ON CEREMONIAL AND CORPORATE OCCASIONS

CHAPTER CONTENT

Discussion Questions

1.   In what way do ceremonial and corporate speeches assist in building a sense of community?
2.   What is one fundamental truism that guides communication in a diverse culture?
3.   What is meant by saying "human beings orient themselves to the world via language?"
4.   How is your sense of group identity constructed?
5.   What is the role of ritual in building community through public presentations?
6.   What is the relationship between this chapter's discussion and that in Ch. 4? How can the material covered in Ch. 4 assist in building speeches for ceremonial and corporate occasions?
7. . What principles should be observed in a speech of introduction?
8.   What situations or audiences require speeches of tribute?
9.   What are three typical speeches of tribute?
10.   What are the primary characteristics of the occasion for a speech of tribute? How can the speaker adapt under these circumstances?
11.   Provide an example of an occasion requiring a speech of goodwill.
12.   What are three guidelines for selecting materials for a goodwill speech?
13.   How should you organize a speech of goodwill?
14.   What are the purposes of a speech to entertain?
15.   How should you select material to include in a speech to entertain?
16.   How can you organize a speech to entertain?
17.   How does humor function in a speech to entertain?
18.   What does a keynote speech require?
19.   What are some ways to prepare for participation in a panel discussion?

Questions to Stimulate Critical Thinking

1.   Can you identify ceremonial or corporate occasions calling for public speeches which are not included in this chapter in your textbook? What are they? Identify what you think are the guidelines for speaking on such occasions.
2.   What is the impact of the occasion in dictating the requirements for speeches on ceremonial or corporate occasions? Is it the most important factor involved in such speeches?
3.   Which situations create special difficulty for the speaker? What determines "good taste" in these situations? Can you provide some guidelines?
4.   Which forms of political speaking have developed into ritualistic or ceremonial occasions? You might consider State of the Union speeches, press conferences, diplomatic visits, etc.
5.   Discuss the nature of group solidarity or membership. How does the feeling of group identity emerge? What is the role of the speaker in creating or crystallizing such

solidarity? Do you think that timing is critical in stimulating feelings of group solidarity? If so, why? If not, what is critical in developing group solidarity?

6. Ceremonial speaking is often considered to be "window dressing." Do you think this is accurate? Why? If this form of speaking goes beyond making audience members feel good, what does it accomplish?

7. What is the relationship between ceremonial speaking and rituals to establish power? You might think of rituals that reinforce group cohesion.

8. What are some examples of ceremonial or corporate occasions you have participated in as a listener or as a speaker?

9. How is humor culturally determined? Investigate the boundaries or rules for humor in our culture. Compare these if you can to another culture.

10. Can you identify fads or cycles in entertainment? What triggers these fads? What kind of entertainment or humor is currently popular? Why do you think it is popular? How did it develop? How can a speaker adapt to changing styles of humor or entertainment?

11. What functions do the keynotes at the Republican and Democratic national conventions play. Which keynote speeches do the students recall as memorable, if any? Why or why not?

12. What are the ethical obligations related to participation in a panel discussion, especially when there is disagreement between and among participants?

Application Exercises

1. The Eulogy
   A. Objective: To offer an opportunity to experience a form of a ceremonial speech.
   B. Procedure: Provide students with copies of eulogies for famous people. Examples might be gathered from anthologies, obituary sections in major newspapers or special issues of news magazines. Read and compare the content and persuasive strategies in each.
   C. Discussion: How does the speaker/writer integrate persuasive and informative functions? Does the speaker/writer create an emotional response in the audience? Could the opposite impact be achieved? How?

2. Competitive Speaking
   A. Purpose: To expose students to excellent examples of ceremonial or corporate speaking by peers.
   B. Procedure: Assign students to attend one or more rounds of competition at a local forensics tournament featuring individual events such as After Dinner Speaking, Rhetorical Criticism, Prose, Poetry, etc. Ask students to take notes and prepare observations on what they say for class.

C. Discussion: Compare students' responses. What characteristics typify these occasions for speaking? What differences were noted? You may wish to compare characteristics of classroom speaking with competitive speaking.

3. Toasting the Occasion

    A. Objective: To provide students with experience developing speeches of goodwill.

    B. Procedure: Identify several occasions students are likely to encounter such as weddings, political victory celebrations, anniversaries, and dedications. Assign teams and ask each team to write an appropriate toast for the occasion. Share the results.

    C. Discussion: Does the toast create goodwill? How? Which strategies for generating goodwill were most effective? Why?

4. The Late Night Monologue

    A. Objective: To apply the principles of speaking to entertain discussed in the textbook.

    B. Procedure: Ask students to watch the opening monologue of a popular late night talk show or bring a tape of a monologue to show in class. Identify the purpose, organizational pattern, audience expectations, and other important elements in this speech to entertain.

    C. Discussion: Identify other forms of speaking to entertain and compare and contrast them with the monologue example.

5. The Keynote Exercise:

    A. Objective: To enhance student knowledge concerning keynote speeches.

    B. Procedure: Play a portion of a well-known or recent keynote at the Republican or Democratic convention. Have students work in small groups to evaluate the nature of the keynote and its role in that particular setting.

    C. Discussion: What is the nature of the keynote? How might a political keynote differ from those presented at academic conferences?

6. The Panel Discussion

    A. Objective: To enhance student awareness of panel participation.

    B. Procedure: Have students work in small groups to prepare a report on some facet of communication -- extending knowledge about the use of PowerPoint, or how to prepare a persuasive speech, etc. Have them present their report in class.

    C. Discussion: What do the students see as the major differences between panel participation and speaking alone in front of the class?

7. Additional Exercise: Ask students to complete the activity described in the Ceremonial Speaking handout at the end of this chapter.

Impromptu Speaking Exercises

1. Eulogizing a Celebrity
    A. Objective: To provide an opportunity to apply the principles of eulogistic speaking.
    B. Procedure: Each student should draw the name of a classmate (or famous personality such as a world leader or Hollywood entertainer) and present a mock impromptu eulogy.

2. Introductions
    A. Objective: To develop tact, brevity, sincerity, and enthusiasm, four key skills in presenting an effective introduction.
    B. Procedure: Prior to the next major speaking assignment, pair students. Ask each student to develop and present an introduction of the main speaker using the elements of a good speech of introduction.

3. Speaking to Entertain
    A. Objective: To acquaint students with the use of humor in a speech.
    B. Procedure: Ask students to think of several of their favorite (clean) jokes. You may give them several days to consider the possibilities. In an impromptu speech, ask students to relate their jokes, observing the elements of appropriateness etc.

4. Panel Participation
    A. Objective: To acquaint students with the experience of participating on a panel where there is controversy.
    B. Procedure: Have groups of students select controversial topics about which there is strong disagreement within the group. Have them present their views in an 'open forum' allowing for disagreement to be expressed. Discuss the student's experience in handling disagreement in an open setting such as this.

Additional Resources

Boehme, Ann J. Planning Successful Meetings and Events: A Take-Charge Assistant Book. NY: Wiley, 1998.

Cates, C. "Eulogies as a Special Occasion Speech." Speech Communication Teacher 10 (1996): 6-7.

Gutgold, Nichola D. "Learning the Role of Speech Communication in Our Community: A Local Politician as a Case Study in the Basic Communication Course," Communication Teacher 16 (2001): 10-11.

Lamansky, M. "Getting to Know my Hero: The Speech of Tribute." Speech Communication Teacher 7 (1993): 10.

McMahon, Tom, Big Meetings Big Results: Strategic Event Planning for Productivity and Profit. Lincolnwood, IL: NTC Publishing Group, 1996.

Sutton, D. "Impromptu Speaking Exercise: Academy Award Acceptance Speeches." <u>Speech Communication Teacher</u> 9 (1994): 15.

Williams, Kathleen, W. and Lynn Rinehart, "Here's a Toast." <u>Speech Communication Teacher</u> 12 (Winter 1997): 4.

CEREMONIAL SPEAKING

In speaking on ceremonial or corporate occasions, speakers frequently draw upon traditional sayings or folk wisdom to enhance their messages. Develop each of the following maxims by explaining what it means and then suggesting how it could be used in a ceremonial or corporate speech.

The race is not alone to the swift.
A long dispute means that both parties are wrong.
A rolling stone gathers no moss.
Don't swap horses in the middle of a stream.
None so blind as those who will not see.
No answer is also an answer.
Necessity is the mother if invention.
A barber learns to shave by shaving fools.
A bird in the hand is worth two in the bush.
You can't steal second with one foot on first.
A burnt child dreads the fire.
A drowning person will catch at a straw.
A good beginning is half the battle.
A light purse makes a heavy heart.
A miss is as good as a mile.
All is not gold that glistens.
We do what we must, and call it by the best names.
An open door may tempt a saint.
Every man, deep down, is a fisherman.
Birds of a feather flock together.
Brevity is the soul of wit.
Don't burn your house to scare the mice.
Do not keep a dog and bark yourself.
Every horse thinks its own load heaviest.
Inside every freshman is a senior struggling to escape.
Friends are a second existence.
Success has ruined many a person.
To teach is to learn twice.

SPEAKING AT CONFERENCES

Have the class construct and run a conference on improving public speaking. The students will organize and publicize the conference, and invite faculty from the Department, as well as graduate students (if the Department has a graduate program), to participate. Students also will participate as panel members. Have them construct the topics or themes that they think should be addressed at the conference. The following issues might be focused on:

1. PowerPoint – how to use this as more than just a visual outline of the presentation.

2. Web Research – when to believe it and when not to.

3. Persuasive Appeals – which ones might work best and why?

4. Enhancing your presentation – besides using PowerPoint, how else might speaker's enhance their speeches?

5. Speaking on controversial topics – what should speakers do in speaking on issues that create strong emotional reactions from some or all audience members (either pro or con with respect to the issue)?

SECTION III: *A SELECTED BIBLIOGRAPHY*

General Resources

Allen, R.R. and Theodore Reuter. <u>Teaching Assistant Strategies: An Introduction to College Teaching</u>. Dubuque, IA: Kendall Hunt, 1990.

Beck, Isabel L. <u>Questioning the Author: An Approach for Enhancing Student Engagement with Text</u>. Newark, Del., USA : International Reading Association, 1997.

Brookfield, Stephen and Stephen Preskill. <u>Discussion as a Way of Teaching: Tools and Techniques for Democratic Classroom</u>. San Francisco, CA: Jossey-Bass, 1999.

Cronin, Michael and Phillip Glenn. "Oral Communication Across the Curriculum in Higher Education: The State of the Art." <u>Communication Education</u> 40 (1991): 356-367.

Daly, John A., Gustav Friedrich, and Anita Vangelisti, Eds. <u>Teaching Communication: Theory, Research, and Methods</u>. Hillsdale, NJ: Lawrence Erlbaum, 1990.

Freiberg, H. Jerome and Amy Driscoll. <u>Universal Teaching Strategies</u>. 3ed Ed., Boston : Allyn & Bacon, 2000.

Ford, W. S. Zabava and Andrew Wolvin. "The Differential Impact of a Basic Communication Course on Perceived Communication Competencies in Class, Work, and Social Contexts." <u>Communication Education</u>, 42 (1993): 215-221.

Gagnon, George W. and Michelle Collay<u>, Designing for Learning: Six Elements in Constructivist Classrooms Thousand</u>. Oaks, CA: Corwin Press, 2001.

Grasha, A. <u>Teaching with Styles: A Practical Guide to Enhancing Learning by Understanding Teaching & Learning Styles</u>. Pittsburgh: Alliance Publishers, 1996.

King, Paul E. and Chris R. Sawyer, "Mindfulness, Mindlessness, and Communication Instruction," <u>Communication Education</u>, (1998), 47, 326-336.

Lee, William, and Diana L. Owens. <u>Multimedia-Based Instructional Design : Computer-Based Training, Web-Based Training, and Distance Learning</u> Jossey-Bass, 2000.

Olson, Kathleen. <u>Something to Talk About : A Reproducible Conversation Resource for Teachers and Tutors</u>. Ann Arbor, MI: University of Michigan Press, 2001.

Resources on Objectives, Criteria, and Power in the Classroom

Buerkel-Rothfuss, Nancy L., Pamela Gray and Janet Yerby.   "The Structured Model of Competency-Based Instruction." <u>Communication Education</u> 42 (1993): 22-36.

Kearney, Patricia, Timothy G. Plax, Virginia P. Richmond, and James C. McCroskey. "Power in the Classroom III: Teacher Communication Techniques and Messages." <u>Communication Education</u> 34 (1985): 19-28.

Lichtenstein, Allen and E. Phil Eftyshiadis. "Student Video Productions: Who Owns the Copyright?" Communication Education 42 (1993): 37-49.

Richmond, Virginia P., James C. McCroskey, Patricia Kearney, and Timothy G. Plax. "Power in the Classroom VII: Linking Behavior Alteration Techniques to Cognitive Learning." Communication Education 36 (1987): 1-12.

Richmond, Virginia P. and James C. McCroskey. "Power in the Classroom II: Power and Learning." Communication Education 33 (1984): 125-136.

Resources on Instructional Strategies and Activities

Bitter, Gary G. and Melissa E. Pierson. Using technology in the classroom. 5th Ed., Boston: Allyn & Bacon, 2002.

Blom, Patricia. "Using Group Activities in Basic Public Speaking." Speech Communication Teacher 4 (1989): 10-11.

Dantonio, Marylou and Paul C. Beisenherz. Learning to Question, Questioning to Learn: Developing Effective Teacher Questioning Practices . Boston: Allyn & Bacon, 2000.

Dantonio, Marylou and Paul C. Beisenherz. Learning to Question, Questioning to Learn: Developing Effective Teacher Questioning Practices. Boston : Allyn and Bacon, 2001.

Koester, Jolene and Myron Lustig. "Communication Curricula in the Multicultural University." Communication Education 40 (1991): 250-254.

Palloff, Rena M. and Keith Pratt. Building Learning Communities in Cyberspace : Effective Strategies for the Online Classroom. San Francisco, CA: Jossey-Bass, 1999.

Palloff, Rena M. and Keith Pratt. Lessons from the Cyberspace Classroom : The Realities of Online Teaching. San Francisco, CA: Jossey-Bass, 2001.

Rosenberg, Marc. J. E-Learning: Strategies for Delivering Knowledge in the Digital Age. NY: McGraw Hill, 2000.

Wellins, R., W. Byam, and J. Wilson. Empowered Teams: Creating Self-Directed Work Groups that Improve Quality, Productivity, and Participation. San Francisco: Jossey-Bass, 1991.

White, Ken W. and Bob H. Weight. (Eds.), Online Teaching Guide, The: A Handbook of Attitudes, Strategies, and Techniques for the Virtual Classroom. Boston: Allyn & Bacon, 1999.

Wilson, Susan R. "The Little Speech That Could," Speech Communication Teacher 13 (Spring 1999): 10-11.

Resources on Assessment of Students

Angelo, T.A. and K. P. Cross. <u>Classroom Assessment Techniques: A Handbook for Faculty</u>, 2nd ed. San Francisco: Jossey-Bass, 1993.

Cross, L. H. , R. Frary, and L. Weber. "College Grading: Achievement, Attitudes and Effort." <u>College Teaching</u>, 41 (1993): 143-152.

Goulden, Nancy and Charles Griffin. "The Meaning of Grades Based on Faculty and Student Metaphors." <u>Communication Education</u> 44 (1995): 110-125.

Johnson, D. W., R. T. Johnson, and R. Holubec. <u>Circles of Learning: Cooperation in the Classroom</u>, 3rd ed. Edina, MN: Interaction Book Company, 1990.

Lowman, J. <u>Mastering the Techniques of Teaching</u>, 3rd ed. San Francisco: Jossey-Bass, 1995.

Seibold, David, Sami Kudsi, and Michael Rude. "Does Communication Training Made a Difference? Evidence for the Effectiveness of a Presentational Skills Program." <u>Applied Communication Research</u> 21 (1993): 11-131.

Wood, Julia T. and Lisa Firing Lenze. "Strategies to Enhance Gender Sensitivity in Communication Education." <u>Communication Education</u> 40 (1991): 16-21.

Resources on Assessment of Instruction

Hay, Ellen. "A National Survey of Assessment Trends in Communication Departments." <u>Communication Education</u> 41 (1992): 247-257.

Jensen, Karla Kay and Vinnie Harris, "The Public Speaking Portfolio," <u>Communication Education</u>, (1999), 48, 211-27.

Murray, J. P. "Better Testing for Better Learning." <u>College Teaching</u>, 38 (1990): 148-152.

Nussbaum, Jon F. "Effective Teacher Behaviors." <u>Communication Education</u> 41 (1992): 167-180.

Richlin, L. and B. Manning. <u>Improving a College/University Teaching Evaluation System: A Comprehensive, Developmental Curriculum for Faculty and Administrators</u>, 2nd ed. Pittsburgh: Alliance Publishers, 1995.

Seldin, Peter. <u>The Teaching Portfolio</u>. Boston: Anker Publishing, 1991.

Audiovisual Resources

Audiovisual materials are not teaching strategies in and of themselves. Rather, they can be used as supplements designed to present information and create understanding. When using audiovisual materials, the same guidelines which govern the use of classroom exercises should be followed. The materials should be prepared ahead of time, previewed adequately for the student, and followed with a discussion, exercise, lecture or reading intended to integrate the material with the goals of the course. It should always be remembered that audiovisual materials serve as aids to teaching, not replacements for it. The following listing is not intended to be exhaustive, but to save time in looking for those companies that produce contemporary videos that might be used in the classroom. The listings under each company are also representative rather than exhaustive.

The Educational Video Group - 291 Southwind Way, Greenwood, IN 46142:
website: http://www.evgonline.com/
> Great Moments from the Great Speeches Cat. # 1022
> Great Speeches: The Video Series [13 videos]
> Great Speeches: Today's Women [2 videos]
> Successful Speaking: Video Series [includes Using Logic and Reasoning, Organizing the
> > Speech, Delivery Techniques, Conquering Communication Anxiety]
> Rohler, Lloyd and Roger Cook Great Speeches for Criticism and Analysis 3rd Ed.
> > [contains 44 speeches and 16 critical essays] Cat. # 1103T
> Weithoff, William E. Writing the Speech [book and video]

Films for the Humanities and Sciences - P. O. Box 2053, Princeton, NJ 08543
> website: http://www.films.com
> Effective Listening Skills
> Constructive Communications
> The Power of Speech
> Doublespeak

GPN - P.O Box 80699, Lincoln, NB 68501
> website: http://gpn.unl.edu
> Speaking With Confidence [24 videos on varied communication topics, such as
> > Critical thinking, presentational aids, critiquing public speeches]

Media Education Foundation - 26 Center Street, Northampton, MA 01060
> website: http://www.mediaed.org
> Dreamworlds II: Desire, Sex, and Power in Music Video
> Lani Guinier: Democracy in a Different Voice
> Stuart Hall on Representation
> Constructing Public Opinion
> Michael Eric Dyson: Material Witness
> Note: While not on public speaking per se, these and other videos from MEF may serve to stimulate discussion about the role of communication in society.